AN ILLUSTRATED DATA GUIDE TO

WORLD WAR II
FIGHTERS

Compiled by
Christopher Chant

TIGER BOOKS INTERNATIONAL
LONDON

c1

This edition published in 1997 by
Tiger Books International PLC
Twickenham

Published in Canada in 1997 by
Vanwell Publishing Limited
St. Catharines, Ontario

© Graham Beehag Books
Christchurch
Dorset

Printed in Hong Kong

ISBN 1-85501-859-4

CONTENTS

Focke-Wulf Fw 190

Manufacturer: Focke-Wulf Flugzeugbau G.m.b.H.

Country of origin: Germany

Specification: Fw 190A-8

Type: Fighter

Accommodation: Pilot in an enclosed cockpit

Entered service: August 1941

Left service: 1948

Operational equipment: Standard communication and navigation equipment, plus a Revi 16/B reflector gunsight

Armament: Two 20mm MG 151/20E fixed forward-firing cannon with 250 rounds per gun in the wing roots with synchronisation equipment to fire through the propeller disc, two 20mm MG 151/20E fixed forward-firing cannon with 140 rounds per gun in the wing leading edges, and two 0.51in (13mm) MG 131 fixed forward-firing machine-guns with 475 rounds per gun in the upper part of the

Fast, agile, strong and well armed, the Focke-Wulf Fw 190 was one of the classic fighters of all time, and probably the finest fighter operated by the Germans in World War II.

forward fuselage with synchronisation equipment to fire
through the propeller disc

Powerplant: One BMW 801D radial piston engine rated
at 1,700hp (1,268kW) for take-off and 1,440hp (1,074kW)
at 18,700ft (5,700m)

Fuel capacity: Internal fuel 115.25 Imp gal (524 litres)
plus provision for 25.3 Imp gal (115 litres) of auxiliary fuel
in an optional rear-fuselage tank; external fuel up to 66
Imp gal (300 litres) in one drop tank

Dimensions: Span 34ft 5.5in (10.506m); aspect ratio 6.03;
area 196.98sq ft (18.30sq m; length 29ft 4.25in (8.95m);
height 12ft 11.5in (3.95m); wheel track 11ft 6in (3.50m)

Weights: Empty 7,652lb (3,471kg) equipped; maximum
take-off 9,656lb (4,380kg)

Performance: Maximum level speed 'clean' 354kt
(408mph; 656km/h) at 20,670ft (6,300m) with GM 1
nitrous oxide boost or 349kt (402mph; 647km/h) at
18,045ft (5,500m) without nitrous oxide boost declining
to 308kt (355mph; 571km/h) at sea level; cruising speed,

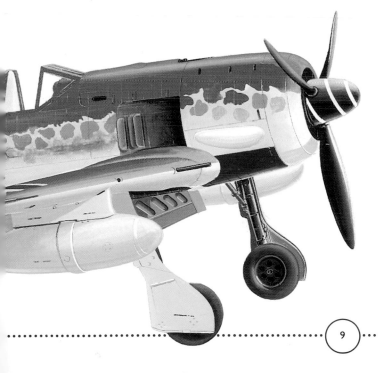

normal 259kt (298mph; 480km/h) at 6,560ft (2,000m); maximum range 795nm (915 miles; 1,472km) with drop tank; typical range 559nm (644 miles; 1,036km) with internal fuel; maximum rate of climb at sea level 3,445ft (1,050m) per minute; climb to 19,685ft (6,000m) in 9min 6sec; service ceiling 37,400ft (11,400m) with GM 1 nitrous oxide boost or 33,795ft (10,300m) without nitrous oxide boost

Variants

Fw 190A-1: The Fw 190 vies with the Messerschmitt Bf 109 for the honour of having been Germany's most important fighter in World War II (1939-45), and when it made its operational debut in the spring of 1941 it was without doubt the finest fighter in the world, comfortably exceeding the capabilities of the Supermarine Spitfire F.Mk V that was its primary adversary and maintaining this superiority until the advent of the Spitfire F.Mk IX a year later. Yet this supreme fighter proved capable of radical development with liquid-cooled inverted-Vee or air-cooled radial piston engines, and was also evolved into an exceptionally potent fighter-bomber and dedicated attack fighter: even in these

As well serving as a conventional air-combat and bomber-interception fighter, the Focke-Wulf Fw 190A was also operated to very good effect in the taxing fighter-bomber role with up to 2205lb (1000 kg) of bombs.

forms the Fw 190 never lost the superb harmonisation of its controls that made it a classic air combat fighter.

The Fw 190 was directionally stable, longitudinally neutral and laterally unstable, and a pilot had at his disposal a positive and highly effective rudder, moderately effective elevators that tended toward heaviness at high speeds, and superbly effective ailerons that remained unaffected by speed and allowed the implementation of exceptionally rapid aileron turns.

The origins of the type can be traced to a 1937 requirement issued by the German air ministry for a single-engined interceptor fighter to supplement the Messerschmitt Bf 109 that had already been selected as the Luftwaffe's standard fighter. Planned by Oberingenieur R. Blaser under the supervision of Dipl.-Ing. Kurt Tank, the new fighter was schemed with a choice of two powerplants, namely the Daimler-Benz DB 601 inverted-Vee piston engine with liquid cooling and the BMW 139 radial piston engine with air cooling. Somewhat to the surprise of all concerned, the German air ministry opted for the radial-engined version for the twin reasons that Daimler-Benz was hard pressed to meet demands for the DB 601, and that the

BMW 139 was already offering a high power output at an excellent power-to-weight ratio and could be expected to offer significant improvements in both factors as its development proceeded. With the new fighter ordered in prototype form, Focke-Wulf began detail design work in the summer of 1938 to finalise the Fw 190 as an aggressive-looking monoplane fighter of cantilever low-wing configuration with a well-streamlined engine installation that included a large ducted spinner designed to improve the nose entry line without detriment to the flow of cooling air needed by the large engine.

The core of the all-metal structure was the fuselage, which was of light alloy construction with a stressed skin of Dural, and this gradually changed in cross-section from circular in the nose section to oval near the tail unit: from front to rear, the fuselage accommodated the powerplant installation and an area of 161.46sq ft (15.00sq m), the Fw 190 V5g introduced an enlarged wing with a span of 34ft 5.5in (10.50m) and an area of 196.99sq ft (18.30sq m). These two prototypes made their maiden flights in the spring of 1940, and it soon became clear that while the larger wing knocked some 5.4kt (6.1mph; 10 km/h) off the maximum level speed it also added significantly to climb rate and manoeuvrability, and it was therefore adopted as the standard wing for the production model. By this time a pre-production batch of 30 Fw 190A-0 fighters had been ordered, and the first nine of these were delivered with the smaller wing.

The larger wing therefore featured on the remaining 21 of the Fw 190A-0 pre-production aircraft, and on the 102 Fw 190A-1 fighters that introduced the type to full production and service even though the initial five were used for test work with the alternative designations Fw 190 V7 to Fw 190 V11. The Fw 190A-1 was modelled closely on the Fw 190 V5g but was powered by the BMW 801C-1 radial, carried an armament of four 0.312in (7.92mm) MG 17 fixed forward-firing machine-guns, had a length of 28ft 10.5in (8.80m), and possessed a maximum take-off weight of 7,066lb (3,205kg). The first unit of the Luftwaffe earmarked for conversion to the new fighter was Jagdgeschwader (JG) 26 based in northern France, and this unit began to convert in March 1941, the Fw 190A-1 reaching operational status in August 1941. The capabilities of the new type were revealed in its first encounter with the Spitfire: for no loss of their own number, the Fw 190A-1s downed three

Spitfires, and the German pilots were able to confirm that while the Spitfire had significantly heavier armament and a better turning radius, the Fw 190A-1 had generally superior agility and indisputably better performance, the latter allowing the German fighter to enter and break off combat on its own terms.

The importance of the Fw 190 in German planning from this time is attested by the fact that while only about 100 examples of the Fw 190A-1 were built, these were delivered from Focke-Wulf, AGO and Arado ñ the first three members of a widespread production effort that was to grow dramatically as the war progressed.

Fw 190A-2: The tactical consequences of the Fw 190A-1's poor firepower had already been foreseen, and the Fw 190A-1 was therefore regarded only as an interim type pending availability of the Fw 190A-2, with the fixed forward-firing armament revised by the replacement of the two 0.312in (7.92mm) MG 17 machine-guns in the wing roots by a pair of 20mm MG FF cannon in the fashion pioneered by the Fw 190 V14 prototype. The cannon certainly increased the Fw 190A-2's weight of fire, but they were drum-fed weapons with a maximum of only 60 rounds per gun. Late aircraft were therefore fitted with supplementary armament in the form of two magazine-fed MG 17 fixed forward-firing machine-guns located farther outboard in the wing leading edges.

The Fw 190A-2 was powered by the improved BMW 801C-2 engine, had additional radio equipment, and, while dimensionally identical to the Fw 190A-1, had a maximum take-off weight of 7,716lb (3,500kg) and a maximum level speed of 337kt (388mph; 625km/h) at 18,045ft (5,500m). The first Fw 190A-2s were delivered to JG 26 in November 1941, and all three of this unit's Gruppen (wings) had converted to the type by April 1942. Production of the Fw 190A-2 totalled 426 aircraft delivered by Focke-Wulf, AGO and Arado.

Fw 190A-3: This may be regarded as the first definitive production model of the Fw 190 series, and was basically similar to the Fw 190A-2 except in its powerplant and armament. In powerplant, the BMW 801C-2 was replaced by the BMW 801D-2 radial engine rated at 1,700hp (1,268kW), and the wing-mounted armament was revised to a quartet of 20mm weapons in the form of two MG FF cannon (in the outboard positions previously occupied by

MG 17 machine-guns in later Fw 190A-2s) and two MG 151/20 cannon (in the inboard positions previously occupied by the MG FF weapons). The MG 151/20 had a significantly higher rate of fire than the MG FF, and was also a belt-fed weapon supplied with ammunition from a large-capacity magazine in the fuselage. Other changes included explosive bolts for the rapid jettisoning of the cockpit canopy in emergencies, and improved protection for the pilot in the form of 0.315 and 0.55in (8 and 14mm) armour plate.

The size and extent of the Fw 190 production programme was now beginning to reveal itself more fully, and although deliveries of the Fw 190A-3 totalled only 509 aircraft, these were delivered in a comparatively short time from the Focke-Wulf factories at Cottbus, Marienburg, Neubrandenburg, Sorau/Silesia, Schwerin and Tutow/Mecklenburg, and from the AGO factory at Oschlersleben, the Arado factories at Brandenburg and Warnem‚nde, and the Fieseler factory at Kassel: an additional 72 aircraft were completed to the slightly revised Fw 190Aa-3 standard and delivered to Turkey in 1942 and 1943. By the spring of 1942, the production rate for the Fw 190 was 250 fighters per month, soon rising to 500 fighters per month as all these facilities increased output.

The Fw 190A-3 was dimensionally identical to the Fw 190A-2, but differed in details such as its empty weight of 6,393lb (2,900kg); maximum take-off weight of 8,377lb (3,800kg); maximum level speed of 332kt (382mph; 615km/h) at 19,685ft (6,000m) declining to 271kt (312mph; 502km/h) at sea level; cruising speed of 241kt (278mph; 447km/h) at optimum altitude;

The Focke-Wulf Fw 190 offered its pilot good fields of vision from its fully glazed cockpit, which was accessed by a rearward-sliding rear portion, and its cockpit was well planned for the fighter role with a central control column, moderately high-set rudder pedals, primary flight and engine instruments on the front panel, and the engine and communication controls on the port and starboard coamings respectively.

maximum range of 432nm (497 miles; 800km); initial climb rate of 2,838ft (865m) per minute, and service ceiling of 34,775ft (10,600m).

Subvariants of the Fw 190A-3, as with other German warplanes, were produced by the addition of Umr‚st-Baus‰otze (factory conversion sets) and R‚sts‰otzc (field conversion sets).

Fw 190A-4: Introduced to service during the summer of 1942, this was basically the Fw 190A-3 with revised radio equipment (necessitating a small antenna mast on the leading edge of the fin), and an uprated powerplant in the form of the standard BMW 801D-2 radial engine revised with the MW 1 methanol/water power-boost system to raise the engine's maximum rating to 2,100hp (1,566kW) for short periods, thereby permitting an increase in maximum level speed to 361kt (416mph; 670km/h) at 20,670ft (6,300m) after take-off at a maximum weight of 8,377lb (3,800kg).

The Fw 190A-4 was also adapted for a number of alternative or supplementary roles by the installation of Umr‚st-Baus‰otze and R‚sts‰otze, indicated by the appropriate suffix to the basic designation. The Fw 190A-4 series, of which 894 were built, continued in production into 1943.

Fw 190A-5: Introduced to service early in 1943, the Fw 190A-5 was a version of the Fw 190A-4 with a revised engine mounting that positioned the BMW 801D-2 engine some 5.9in (0.15m) farther forward (to increase length to 29ft 4.25in/8.95m and restore the centre of gravity to the location it had occupied before its alteration by the addition of extra equipment in the rear fuselage), a maximum take-off weight of 9,480lb (4,300kg), and provision for a larger assortment of Umr‚st-Baus‰otze and R‚sts‰otze. Production of the Fw 190A-5 series by Focke-Wulf, AGO, Arado and Fieseler totalled 723 aircraft.

Fw 190A-6: This was the production-line version of the Fw 190A-5/U10, with a lightened wing structure that was nonetheless able to accommodate a fixed armament of four 20mm MG 151/20 cannon that were supplemented by the two fuselage-mounted 0.312in (7.92mm) MG 17 machine-guns for a maximum take-off weight of 8,598lb (3,900kg). Production of the Fw 190A-6 fighter totalled 569 aircraft, and many of these were converted with Umr‚st-Baus‰otze and R‚sts‰otze.

Fw 190A-7: Entering production in December 1943, the Fw 190A-7 was the production derivative of the Fw 190A-5/U9 with a maximum take-off weight of 8,818lb (4,000kg) and the revised fixed armament of two 20mm MG 151/20 cannon in the wing roots and two 0.51in (13mm) MG 131 machine-guns in the upper part of the forward fuselage, together with a new type of gunsight. Production by Focke-Wulf, AGO, Arado and Fieseler totalled 80 aircraft.

Fw 190A-8: This was the final production model of the Fw 190A-series, and was built from December 1943 in larger numbers than any other Fw 190A-series fighters: production by Focke-Wulf, AGO, Arado and Fieseler totalled 1,334 aircraft. The type was powered by the BMW 801D-2 radial engine in a form with the GM 1 nitrous oxide power-boost system, and its other changes included a 25.3 Imp gal (115 litre) increase in internal fuel capacity through the introduction of a small auxiliary tank in the rear fuselage, different radio equipment, and the underfuselage rack moved 7.9in (0.20m) farther forward.

Such were the capabilities of the Fw 190A-8 that the revived French air force decided to place the type in production during 1945 to bridge the gap until it could acquire or develop more advanced types, and this resulted in the construction of a further 64 NC.900 aircraft in 1945 and 1946 by the SociÈtÈ Nationale de Constructions AÈronautiques du Centre. The aircraft remained in service for only a few years.

Fw 190D-9: As the Fw 190A series of low- and medium-altitude fighters was being produced, three concurrent programmes were undertaken to develop a high-altitude variant: these were the Fw 190B with a turbocharged BMW 801 radial engine, a pressure cabin and a wing of extended area; the Fw 190C with a turbocharged DB 603A inverted-Vee engine, a pressure cabin and a wing of considerably enlarged span and area; and the Fw 190D with a Junkers Jumo 213 inverted-Vee piston engine and a pressure cabin but without an enlarged wing. The last was the least complex of the three programmes and, not surprisingly, proved by far the most successful.

It was only in 1943 that full-scale work on the Fw 190D began, the first prototype for the series being an Fw 190A-0 that was to have become the Fw 190 V17 prototype with a pressure cabin, a wing spanning 40ft 4.25in (12.30m), and a powerplant of one Jumo 213-1001-S engine rated at 1,750hp (1,305kW) for take-off and cooled by an annular radiator that preserved the radial-engined appearance of the Fw 190A series. This machine now became the Fw 190 V17/U1 with a pressure cabin, standard wings, a powerplant of one Jumo 213A-1 engine rated at 1,750hp (1,305kW) for take-off and 1,600hp (1,193kW) at 18,045ft (5,500m), and a fuselage that was lengthened by some 1ft 11.67in (0.60m) in its forward section to accommodate the engine and by 1ft 7.5in (0.50m) in its rear section to improve directional stability even though a larger vertical tail surface was fitted. The Fw 190 V17/U1 first flew in May 1944 and revealed an excellent combination of handling and performance, the latter being especially good at the higher altitudes where the Fw 190A had begun to suffer. The Fw 190 V17/U1 was armed with two 20mm MG 151/20 cannon and two 0.51in (13mm) MG 131 machine-guns, but the weapon fit intended for the Fw 190D series was somewhat heavier and was validated in the Fw 190 V53 and Fw 190 V54 second and third prototypes, which supplemented this core fit with an outer-wing installation of two more MG 151/20 cannon or alternatively two 30mm MK 108 cannon.

The last prototype was the Fw 190 V21 that introduced a new wing whose area was increased to 210.98sq ft (19.60sq m). By this time, demand for the Fw 190D was urgent, and in August 1944 there appeared a pre-production batch of 10 Fw 190D-0 fighters that were produced as conversions from Fw 190A-7 standard. There were no Fw 190D-1ñ190D-8 versions, for it had been decided that the Fw 190D should succeed the Fw 190A-8, and the initial production model was therefore the Fw 190D-9, based on the airframe of the Fw 190A-8 and with the Jumo 213 engine.

The first Fw 190D-9 fighters were fitted with the original type of cockpit canopy, but later examples switched to the slightly bulged canopy that had been developed for the Fw 190F series of attack aircraft and offered better visibility as well as improved aerodynamics. The details of the Fw 190D-9 included standard communication and navigation equipment plus a Revi 16/B reflector gunsight; armament of two 20mm MG 151/20E fixed forward-firing cannon with 250 rounds per gun in the wing roots and with synchronisation equipment to fire through the propeller disc, and two 0.51in (13mm) MG 131 fixed forward-firing machine-guns with 475 rounds per gun in the upper part of the forward fuselage and with synchronisation equipment to fire through the propeller disc, plus up to 551lb (250kg) of disposable stores carried on one hardpoint under the fuselage; powerplant of one Junkers Jumo 213A-1 inverted-Vee piston engine rated at 1,770hp (1,320kW) for take-off and 2,240hp (1,670kW) at altitude with MW 1 water/methanol power boosting; internal fuel capacity of 115.25 Imp gal (524 litres) plus provision for 25.3 Imp gal (115 litres) of auxiliary fuel in an optional rear-fuselage tank; external fuel of up to 66 Imp gal (300 litres) in one drop tank; span of 34ft 5.5in (10.506m) with an aspect ratio of 6.03 and an area of 196.98sq ft (18.30sq m); length of 33ft 5.25in (10.19m); height of 11ft 0.25in (3.36m); empty weight of 7,694lb (3,490kg); normal take-off weight of 9,480lb (4,300kg); maximum level speed of 370kt (426mph; 686km/h) at 21,650ft (6,600m) declining to 310kt (357mph; 574km/h) at sea level; typical range of 451nm (519 miles; 835km) with internal fuel; climb to 19,685ft (6,000m) in 7min 6sec, and service ceiling of 32,810ft (10,000m).

The Fw 190D-9, nicknamed 'Langnasen-Dora' ('long-nose Dora') entered service in the autumn of 1944, initially with III/JG 54 that was used to protect the base on which the Kommando Novotny was based as it worked up to operational pitch with the Messerschmitt Me 262, Germany's first turbojet-powered fighter, and then with I/JG 26 that became operational in October 1944. Such was the enthusiasm of these units' pilots for the Fw 190A, with which they had previously been equipped, that they were initially distrustful of the new type with its liquid-cooled engine. Operational experience soon revealed that distrust to be wholly misplaced, and the Fw 190D-9 was soon regarded as a superb fighter, and indeed probably the best piston-engined fighter to serve with the Luftwaffe in World War II.

Fw 190D-12: The next model to enter production was the Fw 190D-12 definitive ground-attack fighter that supplanted the Fw 190D-9 during February or March 1945 on the production lines operated by Arado and Fieseler. The new model was fitted with a fixed armament of two 20mm MG 151/20 cannon in the wing roots and one 30mm MK 108 cannon between the cylinder banks of the Jumo 213F engine. This engine was fitted with a three-stage supercharger, was rated at 1,750hp (1,305kW) for take-off or 2,060hp (1,536kW) with the MW HD high-pressure methanol/water power-boost system, and was installed under a sheathing of armour designed to protect it from anti-aircraft fire during low-level missions. Only a very few aircraft were completed in the last stages of the war, and it is thought that none of these was used operationally.

Production of the Fw 190D series totalled 674 aircraft, the majority of these being Fw 190D-9 machines.

Hawker Hurricane

Manufacturer: Hawker Aircraft Ltd.

Country of origin: UK

Specification: Hurricane Mk IIC

Type: Fighter and fighter-bomber

Accommodation: Pilot in an enclosed cockpit

Entered service: Late 1937

Left service: Early 1950s

Operational equipment: Standard communication and navigation equipment, plus a reflector gunsight

Armament: Four 20mm Hispano Mk I or Mk II fixed forward-firing cannon with 91 rounds per gun in the wing leading edges, and up to 1,000lb (454kg) of disposable

Although now remembered for the most part as the partner of the Supermarine Spitfire, the Hawker Hurricane was in fact the more important type in the decisive Battle of Britain fought in the summer and early autumn of 1940, for in this campaign the Hurricane fighters of RAF Fighter Command destroyed more German warplanes than all the other British defences combined. The aeroplane illustrated here is an example of the last main variant, the Hurricane Mk IV produced later in World War II for the fighter-bomber role after the type had become obsolete in the pure fighter task.

stores carried on two hardpoints (both under the wings with each unit rated at 500lb/227 kg), and generally comprising two 500 or 250lb (227 or 113kg) bombs, or eight 60lb (27kg) rockets

Powerplant: One Rolls-Royce Merlin XX inverted-Vee piston engine rated at 1,280hp (954kW) for take-off and 1,460hp (1,089kW) at 6,250ft (1,905m)

Fuel capacity: Internal fuel 97 Imp gal (441 litres); external fuel up to 180 Imp gal (818.3 litres) in two 90 Imp gal (409.1 litre) fixed ferry tanks or 45 Imp gal (204.6 litre) drop tanks

Dimensions: Span 40ft 0in (12.19m); aspect ratio 6.20; area 258.00sq ft (23.97sq m); length 32ft 3in (9.83m); height 13ft 3in (4.04m) with the tail down; wheel track 7ft 10in (2.39m)

Weights: Empty 6,577lb (2,983kg) equipped; normal take-off 7,544lb (3,422kg); maximum take-off 8,044lb (3,649kg)

Performance: Maximum level speed 'clean' 284kt

(327mph; 526km/h) at 18,000ft (5,486m); cruising speed 155kt (178mph; 286km/h) at optimum altitude; maximum range 799nm (920 miles; 1,481km) with drop tanks; typical range 399.5nm (460 miles; 740km) with internal fuel; maximum rate of climb at sea level 2,750ft (838m) per minute; climb to 15,000ft (4,572m) in 6min 0sec; service ceiling 35,600ft (10,850m)

Variants
Hurricane Mk I: The first British warplane capable of exceeding 260kt (300mph; 483km/h) in level flight, the Hurricane was the most important fighter available to the RAF at the beginning of World War II, and its greatest distinction came in the Battle of Britain in the summer of 1940 when the Hurricane destroyed more German aircraft than the rest of the British defences combined. The type may have been overshadowed at this time by the exploits of the Supermarine Spitfire, which was generally tasked with the engagement and destruction of the German fighters, but it was the Hurricane that tackled and decimated the formations of German bombers, which were the only warplanes that could destroy the vital British fighter bases, radar stations, communications centres, and urban areas. The Hurricane was thus instrumental in Britain's survival at a time of major German threat, and although the type was already obsolescent in 1941, it continued to play a major part in British air operations until the end of the war.

Later versions of the fighter pioneered the potent fixed forward-firing armament of four 20mm cannon and then the ability to carry two bombs so that the aeroplane could operate in the fighter-bomber role for sweeps into German-occupied north-west Europe. Drop tanks provided additional range, and when the advent of more-modern German fighters (most notably the Focke-Wulf Fw 190A and Messerschmitt Bf 109F) rendered the Hurricane obsolete for northern European operations, the type was still vital to British efforts in North Africa and later in Burma. In these two theatres the Hurricane was outstandingly successful, as it possessed adequate performance in combination with considerable strength for the survival of combat damage, great reliability under adverse conditions, and wide-track main landing gear units that allowed it to operate from primitive airstrips.

The origins of the Hurricane can be traced to the Air Ministry's F.7/30 requirement, which was specifically framed to spur a major technical evolution in British fighter design. The Air Ministry failed in its intention, however, for the designers of the period opted to plan a number of types that secured their advances from the latent exploitation of biplane thinking rather than exploring the new thinking inherent in the monoplane concept. One of the contenders was Hawker, whose design team under the redoubtable Sydney Camm evolved a monoplane version of the classic Fury biplane fighter in 1933, with a powerplant of one Rolls-Royce Goshawk Vee piston engine, a fixed forward-firing armament of four 0.303in (7.7mm) machine-guns, and fixed tailwheel landing gear with main units carrying spatted mainwheels.

In the following year, however, Rolls-Royce released the initial details of a new engine that was currently known as the PV-12 but would later become famous as the Merlin, and Camm adapted his Fury monoplane design to accommodate this more powerful engine, at the same time adding a canopy to the cockpit and revising the landing gear to the fully retractable type with main units of notably wide track. The improved design was known to Hawker as the Hurricane from January 1934 and was then modified to accord with the F.5/34 requirement, and in this form the Hawker design was the basis for the F.36/34 specification that was written around it in August 1934 before a contract for a single prototype was signed in the following month, specifying an armament of four (later eight) machine-guns.

The prototype made its first flight in November 1935, and in its initial trials revealed very good performance as well as thoroughbred handling characteristics. Confident that large-scale orders would soon materialise, Hawker immediately launched plans for the production of an initial 1,000 aircraft. The company's confidence was rewarded in June 1936 with an initial order for 600 aircraft with changes that included the Merlin I engine, a larger ventral radiator installation, absence of tailplane bracing struts, a more heavily framed sliding canopy section, revised main landing gear doors without the hinged segments designed to cover the lower part of each wheel in the retracted position, and a fixed tailwheel partially protected by a small fairing. Shortly after this, Rolls-Royce discontinued development of the Merlin I in favour of the Merlin II, and this delayed the Hurricane Mk I production programme as the forward fuselage had to be revised to accommodate the engine change. Thus it was October 1937 before the first Hurricane

First delivered as the Hurricane Mk I with an armament of eight 0.303in (7.7mm) Browning machine guns, the Hawker Hurricane was steadily improved in offensive gun power first by the increase in the machine gun armament to 12 0.303in (7.7mm) weapons in the Hurricane Mk IIB and then to the standard illustrated here with four 20mm Hispano cannon in the Hurricane Mk IIC.

Mk I off the production line made its maiden flight, and deliveries to No.111 Squadron followed in December.

The initial standard for these Hurricane Mk I fighters included fabric-covered outer wing panels, a Merlin II engine rated at 1,030hp (768kW) at 16,250ft (4,953m) and 970hp (723kW) at 12,250ft (3,734m) and driving a two-blade Watts propeller of the fixed-pitch type, and a windscreen that was not bullet-proof. The type differed dimensionally from the Hurricane Mk IIC in its length of 31ft 5in (9.58m) and height of 12ft 11.5in (3.95m), and in other details such as its maximum level speed of 276kt (318mph; 512km/h) at 17,400ft (5,303m); initial climb rate of 2,050ft (625m) per minute; climb to 20,000ft (6,096m) in 11min 42sec, and service ceiling of 33,400ft (10,180m).

The Watts propeller was clearly obsolescent, especially for climb rate and service ceiling, and was soon replaced by a three-blade de Havilland propeller of the two-pitch type, and later by a three-blade de Havilland or Rotol propeller of the constant-speed type. The three-blade propellers improved performance right through the flight envelope, although only by a relatively small amount except in climb and service ceiling, and was later used in conjunction with the Merlin III engine that was rated identically to the Merlin II but had a standardised shaft that could carry the de Havilland or Rotol propeller without modification. This engine was standardised for the second production batch, which comprised 300 aircraft with a bullet-proof

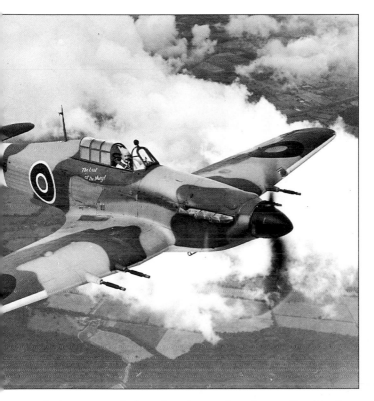

windscreen as their only other major change. By this time, Camm had decided on a switch from fabric-covered outer wing panels to more-modern panels with a skinning of stressed metal. Such wings had first been tested in July 1935 and first flown in April 1939, and were now introduced during the construction of the second batch of Hurricane Mk Is on a piecemeal basis until production could be matched with that of the rest of the airframe.

The first metal-winged Hurricane Mk I was delivered in September 1939, some four weeks after the outbreak of World War II. Both Hawker and the Air Ministry were confident that they were supplying the RAF with a truly effective fighter for the defence of Britain, and now turned their attention to the introduction of armour to protect the pilot (first introduced in February 1940) and the development of heavier firepower. Here, the three options were the adoption of a larger battery of medium machine-guns, the change of the existing battery to heavy machine-guns, or a switch to a smaller battery of cannon firing explosive shells. For logistic reasons the Air Ministry did not want to adopt the heavy machine-gun, and therefore decided in the short term on a larger battery of medium machine-guns while undertaking further investigation of the cannon, which was currently a comparatively unreliable weapon supplied with ammunition from a 60-round drum.

On the outbreak of war in September 1939, the RAF had received 497 Hurricane Mk Is, and most of these provided the operational equipment of 18 first-line fighter squadrons. Many of the aircraft were lost in the Battle of France (May and June 1940), but such was the pace of re-equipment and production that, in July 1940, RAF Fighter Command had 26 Hurricane squadrons (including three that were only partially operational and four that were re-equipping) while in August there were 32 fully operational squadrons and deliveries had exceeded 2,300 aircraft.

The definitive version of the Hurricane Mk I had an armament of eight 0.303in (7.7mm) Browning machine-guns with 334 rounds per gun; empty weight of 5,085lb (2,306kg); normal take-off weight of 6,532lb (2,963kg); maximum take-off weight of 6,661lb (3,021kg); maximum level speed of 281kt (324mph; 521km/h) at 16,250ft (4,953m) declining to 221kt (254mph; 409km/h) at sea level; maximum cruising speed of 236kt (272mph; 438km/h) at 15,000ft (4,572m); economical cruising speed of 152kt (175mph; 282km/h) at 15,000ft (4,572m); maximum range of 782nm (900 miles; 1,448km) with external ferry fuel; typical range of 386.5nm (445 miles; 716km) with internal fuel; initial climb rate of 2,300ft (701m) per minute; climb to 15,000ft (4,572m) in 6min 18sec; and service ceiling of 33,200ft (10,120m). Production of the Hurricane Mk I totalled 3,759 aircraft, comprising 1,900 (some completed as Hurricane Mk IIA aircraft) by Hawker, 1,819 by Gloster, and 40 by Canadian Car & Foundry.

Hurricane Mk IIA: With the Hurricane Mk I in full production, during 1939 the Hawker design team was able to turn to the consideration of a version with heavier armament and improved performance. Both these features demanded the adoption of a higher-rated powerplant; Camm and his team selected a Merlin in the uprated form of the Merlin XX that was initially projected at a rating of 1,185hp (884kW) but delivered at a rating of 1,280hp (954kW), fitted with a two-stage supercharger for improved performance and altitude, and designed specifically for mass production.

The Hurricane variant planned around this engine was the Hurricane Mk II, which was also to incorporate the various improvements (such as three-blade propeller of the constant-speed type, improved armour, and bullet-proof windscreen) that had been introduced successively on the Hurricane Mk I. It was also planned that the Hurricane Mk II should include the improved armament, initially in the form of twelve 0.303in (7.7mm) Browning machine-guns and later in the form of four 20mm Hispano cannon.

However, Birmingham Small Arms could scarcely keep up with current demand for the Browning machine-gun, and in the short term there was no possibility of boosting deliveries to Hawker by 50 per cent. Thus the first Hurricane Mk II aircraft were delivered from September 1940 in the Hurricane Mk IIA Series 1 form with the same armament as the Hurricane Mk I. From October the production standard changed to the Hurricane Mk IIA Series 2, with provision for the original eight-gun wing to be replaced by later wing sets, and with the fuselage lengthened to 32ft 2.5in/9.82m (to facilitate subsequent upgrades) and fitted with strengthened lower longerons to support the weight of the later wing sets. In other respects the Hurricane Mk IIA differed from the Hurricane Mk IIC in details such as its empty weight of 5,500lb (2,495kg); normal take-off weight of 6,000lb (3,005kg), maximum take-off weight of 7,100lb (3,221kg); maximum level speed of 297kt (342mph; 550km/h) at 22,000ft (6,705m) declining to 280kt (322mph; 518km/h) at 13,500ft (4,115m); cruising speed of 184kt (212mph; 341km/h) at optimum altitude; maximum range of 825nm (950 miles; 1,529km) with external fuel; typical range of 408nm (470 miles; 756km) with internal fuel; climb to 20,000ft (6,096m) in 8min 36sec, and service ceiling of 36,300ft (11,065m).

Hurricane Mk IIB: It was in January 1940 that Camm put forward the definitive proposal for a Hurricane variant with the fixed forward-firing armament increased from eight to twelve 0.303in (7.7mm) Browning machine-guns with 332 rounds per gun, and in April of the same year the Air Ministry approved the concept in the form of strengthened outer wing panels that each carried six of the guns as well as a hardpoint rated at 500lb (227kg) and able to carry a bomb or a drop tank. As noted above, a shortage of guns delayed the implementation of the scheme for the 12-gun wing, and it was 1941 before this Hurricane Mk IIB entered service. The Hurricane Mk IIB was dimensionally identical to the Hurricane Mk IIC but differed in details such as its empty weight of 5,640lb (2,558kg); maximum take-off weight of 8,250lb (3,742kg); maximum level speed of 295kt (340mph; 547km/h) at optimum altitude; maximum range of 816nm (940 miles; 1,513km) with external fuel; typical range of 408nm (470 miles; 756km) with internal fuel; climb to 20,000ft (6,096m) in 8min 54sec, and service ceiling of 36,000ft (10,972m).

Hurricane Mk IIC: This was the counterpart of the Hurricane Mk IIB with the fixed forward-firing armament changed to four 20mm Hispano cannon. Like the Hurricane Mk IIB, the Hurricane Mk IIC entered service in 1941 and was operated in the same fighter-bomber role. The last Hurricane to be delivered by the British production programme was a Hurricane Mk IIC that was completed by Hawker in September 1944, ending the programme after the delivery of 12,780 aircraft excluding Belgian and Canadian production. The Hurricane Mk IIC was one of the variants that was exported in modest numbers after World War II, when several countries took this obsolescent type into service.

Hurricane Mk IID: By the middle of 1941, the Air Ministry and Hawker agreed that the Hurricane was obsolete for the pure fighter role, and that future development should be concentrated on exploitation of the Hurricane fighter-bomber and ground-attack capabilities. This led to the evolution of the Hurricane Mk IID, intended specifically for the tank-busting role, with the armament restricted to a pair of 40mm cannon under the wings in an installation that was aimed by registration of the fire of two 0.303in (7.7mm) Browning machine-guns in the leading edges of the wing. The cannon were initially a pair of Rolls-Royce BF weapons with 12 rounds per gun, but these were later replaced by two Vickers 'S' weapons with 15 rounds per gun.

The first Hurricane Mk IID flew in September 1941, and another significant change incorporated in the production model was increased armour protection for the pilot, engine and radiator. The Hurricane Mk IID was most extensively operated in North Africa, where the type entered operational service during June 1942 in the hands of No.6 Squadron. The Hurricane Mk IID proved to be an effective anti-tank weapon, and otherwise differed from the Hurricane Mk IIC in details such as its empty weight of

5,700lb (2,586kg); normal take-off weight of 7,700lb (3,493kg); maximum take-off weight of 8,100lb (3,674kg); maximum level speed of 280kt (322mph; 518km/h) at optimum altitude; maximum range of 782nm (900 miles; 1,448km) with external fuel; typical range of 365nm (420 miles; 676km) with internal fuel; climb to 20,000ft (6,096m) in 12min 24sec, and service ceiling of 32,100ft (9,785m).

The designation Hurricane Mk III was not used as it was reserved for a British-built variant with a Merlin engine made under license in the United States.

Hurricane Mk IV: Making its debut in 1943, initially with the designation Hurricane Mk IIE that was used for the first 270 aircraft, this was the final British production model and was essentially the Hurricane Mk II with the Merlin 24 or 27 engine rated at 1,620hp (1,208kW) at optimum altitude, with 350lb (159kg) of additional armour protection, and with the

Among the many virtues of the Hawker Hurricane were great structural strength, nicely balanced controls, wide-track main landing gear units that provided considerable stability on the ground, and heavy armament that was finalised as four 20mm cannon and either eight 60lb (27kg) rockets or two 500lb (227 kg) bombs.

so-called Universal Wing: this last feature was fitted with two 0.303in (7.7mm) Browning machine-guns and had undersurface provision for two 40mm cannon, or two bombs of up to 500lb (227kg) in wight, or Small Bomb Carriers, or eight air-to-surface rocket projectiles each carrying a 60lb (27kg) warhead, or two smoke-laying installations.

The type entered production early in 1943, and the first machine off the production line made its maiden flight in March of that year. Production totalled 524 aircraft excluding the 270 Hurricane Mk IIE aircraft, and these machines proved especially useful in the Italian and Burmese theatres. The Hurricane Mk IV was the last model to remain in British service, the final aircraft being retired in 1946.

Hurricane Mk X: After delivering 40 Hurricane Mk I aircraft identical to their British counterparts, Canadian Car & Foundry switched to the Hurricane Mk X that was basically similar to the Hurricane Mk IIB except for its powerplant of one Packard (Rolls-Royce) Merlin 28 engine rated at 1,300hp (969kW) and driving a three-blade Hamilton Standard metal propeller of the constant-speed type. This variant was visually distinguishable from the Hurricane Mk IIC by its lack of a propeller spinner. Production of the Mk X totalled 489 aircraft.

Hurricane Mk XI: This was a derivative of the Hurricane Mk X with Canadian rather than RAF equipment, and production totalled 150 aircraft.

Hurricane Mk XII: First flown in November 1941, this was the Canadian equivalent of the Hurricane Mk II, with a powerplant of one Packard Merlin 29 engine rated at 1,300hp (969kW) and driving a three-blade Hamilton Standard metal propeller of the constant-speed type without a spinner. The Hurricane Mk XII, of which 248 were built, originally had an armament of twelve 0.303in (7.7mm) machine-guns that were sometimes replaced in Britain by four 20mm cannon, while the Hurricane Mk XIIA subvariant, of which 150 were built, had the original type of eight-gun armament that was generally replaced by 12 machine-guns or four cannon.

Messerschmitt Bf 109

Manufacturer: Messerschmitt A.G.

Country of origin: Germany

Specification: Bf 109G-6

Type: Fighter and fighter-bomber

Accommodation: Pilot in an enclosed cockpit

Entered service: April 1937

Left service: 1967

Operational equipment: Standard communication and navigation equipment, plus a Revi C/12D reflector gunsight

Armament: One 30mm MK 108 fixed forward-firing cannon with 60 rounds or one 20mm MG 151/20 fixed forward-firing cannon with 150 rounds in a moteur-canon installation and two 0.51in (13mm) MG 131 fixed forward firing machine-guns with 300 rounds per gun in the upper part of the forward fuselage with synchronisation equipment to fire through the propeller disc, and up to 551lb (250kg) of disposable stores carried on one hardpoint under the fuselage, and generally comprising one 551lb (250kg) bomb

Powerplant: One Daimler-Benz DB 605AM inverted-Vee piston engine rated at 1,475hp (1,100kW) for take-off and 1,355hp (1,010kW) at 18,700ft (5,700m)

Fuel capacity: Internal fuel 88 Imp gal (400 litres); external fuel up to 66 Imp gal (300 litres) in one drop tank

Dimensions: Span 32ft 6.5in (9.92m); aspect ratio 6.11; area 173.30sq ft (16.10sq m); length 29ft 0.5in (8.85m); height 8ft 2.5in (2.50m)

Weights: Empty 5,893lb (2,673kg) equipped; normal take-off 6,940lb (3,148kg); maximum take-off 7,496lb (3,400kg)

Performance: Maximum level speed 'clean' 335kt (386mph; 621km/h) at 22,640ft (6,900m) declining to 295kt (340mph; 547km/h) at sea level; cruising speed, maximum 286kt (330mph; 531km/h) at 19,030ft (5,800m); maximum range 410nm (621 miles; 1,000km) with drop tank; typical range 304nm (350 miles; 563km) with internal fuel; maximum rate of climb at sea level 3,346ft (1,020m) per minute; climb to 18,700ft (5,700m) in 6min 0sec; service ceiling 37,890ft (11,548m)

Variants

Bf 109E-1: The 'Emil' was the most important version of the Bf 109 family of classic fighters available to the Luftwaffe in the early years of World War II, and was instrumental in the Luftwaffe's success in winning and then retaining air superiority over the Polish, Scandinavian and North-West European battlefields between September 1939 and June 1940. It was only when the type was committed at longer range against the warplanes of the RAF's Fighter Command in the Battle of Britain (during the summer of 1940) that the type's limitations began to be appreciated.

The origins of the Bf 109 can be traced to 1933 and as the result of a bitter feud between Erhard Milch, the state secretary of aviation, and Dipl.-Ing. Willy Messerschmitt. This feud had its origins in 1929 when Milch, then managing director of Deutsche Lufthansa, cancelled the airline's order for 10 Bayerische Flugzeugwerke (BFW) M-20b transports, which were almost complete, and demanded the repayment of the deposit paid for these aircraft. BFW could not afford to make the payment and was forced into a bankruptcy from which it emerged with considerable difficulty as Milch (now state secretary of aviation and deputy to Hermann Gˆring, the minister for aviation and head of the Luftwaffe) made it clear that he expected the company to concentrate its efforts on the licensed production of other companies' products. Messerschmitt was determined to continue with the aircraft of his own design and, in the absence of German orders, began to solicit foreign interest in BFW's capabilities. This enterprise was rewarded during 1933 by Romanian orders, but these successes incensed Milch, who arranged for the German air ministry to castigate BFW for concentrating on foreign orders rather than German interests. This reaction was just what Messerschmitt and his co-manager, Rakan Kokothaki, had been awaiting, for it gave the two men the opportunity to state publicly that BFW was seeking foreign orders only because it could not secure domestic support or domestic orders.

This forced the hand of the German air ministry, which now instructed Messerschmitt to complete six examples of his M-37 design for entry as Bf 108A machines in the 4th

As revealed by the two markings on the side of the fuselage, this is a Messerschmitt Bf 109E-3 fighter of the 9.Staffel (squadron) of the Jagdgeschwader 26 "Schlageter" fighter group's III Gruppe (wing) based in northern France during the Battle of Britain. Noteworthy features of the design are the narrow track of the outward-retracting main landing gear units and the side-hinged access section for the cramped cockpit.

Challenge de Tourisme Internationale competition to be held near Z̤rich during August and September 1934. Under air ministry instructions, and after the crash of one of the machines, several German pilots complained that the Bf 108A was dangerous. Messerschmitt was able to show convincingly that the type was structurally and aerodynamically safe, however, and in the 1934 competition the Bf 108A took fifth and sixth places and, more importantly, revealed that it was also the fastest of all the competitors as a result of its clean design as a cantilever low-wing monoplane with retractable main landing gear units. Messerschmitt had now been joined by Dipl.-Ing. Walther Rethel in the capacity of chief engineer, and it was under the leadership of Messerschmitt and Rethel that the Bf 108A was transformed into the Bf 108B Taifun four-seat cabin monoplane that was soon winning significant orders.

Meanwhile, the two men had also been collaborating on the preliminary design of a single-seat fighter after the German air ministry had been forced to include BFW with Arado, Focke-Wulf and Heinkel when awarding development contracts for the first 'modern' fighter planned for Luftwaffe service. The type received the official designation Bf 109, and inherited from the Bf 108 its basic configuration as a cantilever low-wing monoplane as well as other important features.

In historical terms, the Bf 109 was a milestone as it was the first warplane to combine in one airframe a number of features that had otherwise appeared only individually or in pairs on other aircraft: these features included an all-metal structure (first used on the Dornier Do H Falke fighter of 1922), stressed-metal skinning (first used in the Short Silver Streak of 1920), a metal semi-monocoque fuselage structure (used in several fighters of the 1920s), leading-edge automatic slots and trailing-edge slotted flaps (first used on the Handley Page H.P.21 of 1923), and the combination of an enclosed cockpit and retractable main landing gear units (used on the Grumman carrierborne fighters of the early 1930s). Combined in the Bf 109, they gave a sleek appearance to a design based on an oval-section fuselage with a side-hinged canopy whose rear edge was faired into the upper line of the raised rear fuselage, a plain tail unit with the strut-braced horizontal surface located about one-quarter of the way up the vertical surface, and a cantilever low-set wing that was dihedraled and also tapered in thickness and chord. Other features included an armament

Seen in desert markings and fitted with a sand filter over its carburettor inlet, this is a Messerschmitt Bf 109E of the I Gruppe of Jagdgeschwader 27 serving in North Africa.

of two 0.312in (7.92mm) MG 17 fixed forward-firing machine-guns installed in the upper part of the forward fuselage with synchronisation equipment to fire through the propeller disc, provision for the installation of either of the two new 12-cylinder Vee piston engines under development as the Daimler-Benz DB 600 and Junkers Jumo 210 series, the strength to cope with German air ministry demands for very high turn and roll rates, the ability to undertake a maximum-power dive, and excellent spinning characteristics without any tendency to enter a flat and unrecoverable spin.

The construction of prototype aircraft had begun late in 1934, and the Bf 109 V1 (at first Bf 109a) initial prototype made its maiden flight in September 1935 with a powerplant (in the continued absence of the planned Jumo 210) of one Rolls-Royce Kestrel V Vee piston engine rated at 695hp (518kW) for take-off and 640hp (477kW) at 14,000ft (4,267m), and driving a two-blade Schwarz wooden propeller of the fixed-pitch type. After the completion of manufacturer's trials, the Bf 109 V1 was submitted for official trials, but encountered considerable resistance from pilots who disliked the fighter's nose-high attitude on the ground, leading-edge slots, narrow-track main landing gear units, and high wing loading.

With the Arado Ar 80 V1 and Focke-Wulf Fw 159 V1 soon eliminated from the running, the rival Heinkel He 112 V1 thus emerged from the first stage of the trials as the test pilots' favourite despite the fact that the Bf 109 V1 had recorded a maximum level speed of 251kt (289mph; 465km/h), which was some 17 per cent greater than the

speed revealed by the He 112 V1, together with higher climb and dive speeds: against these obvious advantages the test pilots preferred the He 112 V1's wider-track main landing gear units, its better fields of vision for take-off and landing, and its lower wing loading. The Bf 109 V1 was joined in the test programme during January 1936 by the Bf 109 V2 with the Jumo 210A inverted-Vee engine rated at 610hp (455kW) for take-off, and in June 1936 by the Bf 109 V3 that differed from the Bf 109 V2 in having the fuselage-mounted armament of two MG 17 machine-guns. There followed a batch of 10 pre-production aircraft, and by the time of the competitive fly-off between the Bf 109 and He 112 in the autumn of 1936, the BFW fighter was the decided favourite to secure a major production order, and at the end of the fly-off it was ordered into production.

By this time there were worries about the Bf 109's inferiority in armament to both the new British 'modern' fighters, namely the first-generation Hawker Hurricane and second-generation Spitfire, and it was decided that the Bf 109B-0 pre-production aircraft should be completed with three 0.312in (7.92mm) MG 17 machine-guns, the third weapon being added in the angle between the engine's cylinder banks and firing through the hollow propeller shaft. The 10 aircraft were all used for development work with Versuchs (experimental) numbers. The Bf 109 entered full production as the Bf 109B-1 during the autumn of 1936, by

This Messerschmitt Bf 109E is identified as a machine of the II Gruppe of Jagdgeschwader 3 "Udet" by the shield marking on the side of the fuselage just forward of the cockpit and the horizontal black bar to the rear of the cross, and as the Gruppe adjutantis aeroplane by the black chevron forward of the cross.

which time BFW had been reorganised as Messerschmitt A.G., and this first operational variant entered service in April 1937. It had been planned that the type should enter service first with the II Gruppe of Jagdgeschwader (JG) 132 'Richthofen' in Germany, but by this time the USSR had supplied the Spanish Republican government forces with Polikarpov I-15 biplane and I-16 monoplane fighters. These both revealed a clear advantage over the Heinkel He 51 biplane fighters currently equipping Jagdgruppe 88 of the Legion Condor, as the German expeditionary air arm was designated. After rapid conversion on the new fighter, therefore, personnel of II/JG 132 were posted to Spain as the 2.Staffel of Jagdgruppe 88. The Bf 109B-1 soon revealed a marked superiority over the I-15 and I-16, and this superiority was retained and improved by later versions of the fighter.

These later subvariants included the Bf 109B-2, with the original type of two-blade wooden propeller of the fixed-pitch type, later replaced by a three-blade VDM (Hamilton Standard) metal propeller of the constant-speed type for much improved all-round performance; and the Bf 109C-1, with a deeper radiator bath under the forward fuselage for the Jumo 210Ga inverted-Vee engine, and with the armament revised to four 0.312in (7.92mm) MG 17 machine-guns installed as two weapons with 500 rounds per gun in the upper part of the forward fuselage and two weapons with 420 rounds per gun in the wing leading edges. The first variant not to see service in the Spanish Civil War (1936-39) was the Bf 109C-2 with the engine-mounted MG 17 machine-gun restored to provide a forward-firing battery of five 0.312in (7.92mm) weapons. This model was to have been supplemented by the Bf 109C-3 with the engine-mounted MG 17 replaced by a 20mm MG FF/M cannon, but the few aircraft built were retained for development purposes.

The next variant to appear was the Bf 109D, which was considered an interim type pending the availability of the first definitive model, the Bf 109E with the DB 601 inverted-Vee engine. The Bf 109D was powered by the DB 600Aa inverted-Vee engine rated at 986hp (735kW) for take-off and 910hp (679kW) at 13,125ft (4,000m), and offered a much higher level of performance than the Jumo 210-engined Bf 109B and Bf 109C. After the delivery of a small number of Bf 109D-0 pre-production fighters, the only subvariant of the Bf 109D series to enter service was the Bf 109D-1 with strengthened wings, stronger main landing gear unit attachments, and an armament of one 20mm MG FF/M cannon in a moteur-canon installation with 160 rounds and two 0.312in (7.92mm) MG 17 machine-guns with 500 rounds in the upper part of the forward fuselage. The MG FF/M was an indifferent weapon, and was often removed so that the armament was represented by two machine-guns with the enlarged ammunition capacity of 1,000 rounds per gun.

The last operator of the Messerschmitt Bf 109E series was the Spanish air force, which flew the type as a first-line fighter and then as an advanced trainer right from the late 1930s into the 1950s with these interesting markings.

The Bf 109D-2 would have introduced two wing-mounted 0.312in (7.92mm) MG 17 machine-guns that were to have been replaced in the Bf 109D-3 by two MG FF cannon, but neither subvariant entered service as the German air ministry decided to concentrate on the Bf 109E series, which was Germany's most important fighter on the outbreak of World War II.

From the beginning of the Bf 109 programme, it had been envisaged that the type would eventually be fitted with the Daimler-Benz DB 600 series of inverted-Vee piston engines, and the first prototype to have this powerplant was the Bf 109 V10 that made its maiden flight in July 1937 with a DB 600Aa inverted-Vee engine driving a three-blade VDM metal propeller of the constant-speed type. There followed a number of other DB 600-powered prototypes and the Bf 109D production model itself before the advent of the Bf 109 V14 and Bf 109 V15 that introduced the definitive powerplant of one DB 601A-1 inverted-Vee engine, rated at 1,050hp (783kW) for take-off and fitted with a fuel-injection system in place of the DB 600's standard carburettor. The fuel-injection system allowed pilots to undertake negative-g manoeuvres without fear of the engine cutting out. After the delivery of 10 Bf 109E-0 pre-production aircraft with a powerplant of one DB 601A-1 engine and an armament of four 0.312in (7.92mm) MG 17 fixed forward-firing machine-guns, the Bf 109E-1 entered service in February 1939 with the same powerplant but with the armament revised to two 20mm MG FF cannon with 60 rounds per gun in the wing leading edges and two 0.312in (7.92mm) machine-guns with 1,000 rounds per gun in the upper part of the forward fuselage. Initial deliveries were made to units in Germany and, despite the feeling that the Spanish Civil War was at a close, to Jagdgruppe 88.

The Bf 109E-1/B was a fighter-bomber conversion evolved in the summer of 1940 with provision under the fuselage for one 551lb (250kg) bomb although, for range reasons, it was more common to carry a single 110lb (50kg) bomb.

Bf 109E-3: This was the development of the Bf 109E-1 with the DB 601Aa inverted-Vee engine rated at 1,175hp (876kW) for take-off, and included provision for the inclusion of one 20mm MG FF/M fixed forward-firing cannon in a moteur-canon installation (if the machine-gun ammunition was reduced in quantity), a revised canopy and, for the first time in any Bf 109 variant, armour protection for the pilot.

Bf 109E-4: Appearing late in 1939 for service from the summer of 1940, this was a development of the Bf 109E-3 with all provision for the MG FF/M cannon removed and the MG FF cannon in the wings changed to a version with a high rate of fire. The Bf 109E-4/B was the fighter-bomber version evolved in the summer of 1940, with provision for a maximum 551lb (250kg) bomb load in the form of one 551lb (250kg) bomb or four 110lb (50kg) bombs. The other details of the Bf 109E-4 included an armament of two 20mm MG FF fixed forward-firing cannon with 60 rounds per gun in the wing leading edges and two 0.312in (7.92mm) MG 17 fixed forward-firing machine-guns with 1,000 rounds per gun in the upper part of the forward fuselage with synchronisation equipment to fire through the propeller disc; a powerplant of one DB 601Aa inverted-Vee piston engine rated at 1,175hp (876kW) for take-off and 1,000hp (746kW) at 12,140ft (3,700m); internal fuel capacity of 88 Imp gal (400 litres); span of 32ft 4.5in (9.87m) with an aspect ratio of 6.025 and an area of 174.05sq ft (16.17sq m); length of 28ft 4.5in (8.64m); height of 8ft 2.33in (2.50m); empty weight of 4,685lb (2,125kg); maximum take-off weight of 5,875lb (2,665kg); maximum level speed of 302kt (348mph; 560km/h) at 14,560ft (4,438m) declining to 252kt (290mph; 467km/h) at sea level; maximum cruising speed of 260.5kt (300mph; 483km/h) at 13,125ft (4,000m); economical cruising speed of 175kt (202mph; 325km/h) at 3,280ft (1,000m); maximum range of 356nm (410 miles; 660km); maximum rate of climb at sea level of 3,280ft (1,000m) per minute; climb to 19,685ft (6,000m) in 7min 45sec, and service ceiling of 34,450ft (10,500m).

Bf 109E-5: This was the reconnaissance fighter derivative of the Bf 109E-4, with the two wing-mounted cannon removed and one Rb 50/30 camera installed in the fuselage immediately to the rear of the cockpit.

Bf 109E-6: This was a development of the Bf 109E-5 with the DB 601N inverted-Vee engine rated at 1,200hp (895kW) for take-off.

Bf 109E-7: This was the version of the Bf 109E-4/N with its underfuselage hardpoint revised for the carriage of bombs (either one 551lb/250kg weapon or four 110lb/50kg weapons) or alternatively a 66 Imp gal (300 litre) drop tank.

Bf 109E-8: This was the development of the Bf 109E-7 with the DB 601E engine rated at 1,350hp (1,007kW) for take-off.

Bf 109E-9: This was the reconnaissance fighter derivative of the Bf 109E-8 with no wing cannon and a camera installation that could comprise one Rb 50/30 or two Rb 32/7 units. The last of these aircraft were completed early in 1942, ending production of the Bf 109E series after the delivery of 4,000 or more aircraft.

Bf 109F-1: The 'Friedrich' marked the apogee of the Bf 109 fighter's development in terms of its aerodynamic qualities and handling characteristics, but these refinements were achieved only at the expense of armament, which was generally considered to be too light for genuine effectiveness. It was for this reason that production of the Bf 109F was terminated after the delivery of only 2,200 aircraft. The Messerschmitt design team had decided in early 1940 (when the Bf 109E was still relatively new in operational terms) that the British and the French would inevitably seek to counter this mainstay of the German fighter arm with improved versions of the Supermarine Spitfire, Bloch MB.151/152 and Dewoitine D.520. France was knocked out of the war in June 1940 before she could field any improved fighters, but the British responded to the Bf 109E by introducing the Spitfire Mk V with the Rolls-Royce Merlin 45 engine using a two-stage supercharger. The Luftwaffe was ready for this development, however, and was able to start operating the improved Bf 109F from March 1941, initially in the hands of JG 2 and JG 26 operating from bases on the southern side of the English Channel.

The Bf 109F had been designed with the aerodynamic refinements that would allow the full exploitation of the greater power promised by the latest version of the DB 601 inverted-Vee piston engine, namely the DB 601E rated at 1,350hp (1,007kW) for take-off. Research had shown that one of the main drag burdens suffered by the Bf 109E was associated with the two underwing radiators for the engine coolant, and the decision was taken to recess these units further into the wing of the Bf 109F with a boundary-layer bypass system to collect the turbulent air from the

The Bf 109F was without doubt the finest variant of the Messerschmitt Bf 109 series in terms of its combination of handling and performance, but was produced only in modest numbers because of pilot criticism of its light armament.

undersurface of the wing immediately ahead of the radiators, channel it over the top of the radiators, and then exhaust it through a duct in the upper part of the inboard flap section, which was split into upper and lower parts: both parts acted together in conjunction with the outer flap section as conventional flaps, but the upper and lower parts of the inner section were also controlled separately by a thermostat and would move apart as the coolant temperature rose, the lower part then serving as a radiator flap. Other changes to the wing, which was slightly reduced in span, included a reduction in the span of the leading-edge slots and trailing-edge ailerons (although the latter were increased in chord so that their area remained unaltered), and the removal of the interlink between the flaps and ailerons.

This was not the limit to the changes introduced in the Bf 109F, however, for the engine cowling was deepened and given a more symmetrical shape whose lines were continued forward by the larger and more curved spinner for the improved propeller of reduced diameter, the supercharger air inlet was moved farther out from the port side of the nose for greater ram effect, the fixed vertical tail surface was improved with a cambered section rather than a symmetrical section for reduced rudder demand in the climb, the rudder was reduced in area, the horizontal tail surface was modified as a cantilever and strutless unit in a position slightly lower and farther forward than on the Bf 109E, the tailwheel was made semi-retractable, and the main landing gear units were raked slightly farther forward. The result of these changes was to reduce the Bf 109F's drag burden by a significant degree, and in combination with the more powerful DB 601E engine this offered the promise of significantly improved performance and better handling through all parts of the flight envelope.

The new fighter was preceded by the Bf 109 V21 and Bf 109 V22 first and second prototypes: the former retaining the DB 601Aa inverted-Vee engine of the Bf 109E but possessing the full package of aerodynamic improvements as well as a 1ft 11.65in (0.60m) reduction in wing span, and the latter introducing the DB 601E engine. Trials revealed that the reduction in span had an adverse effect on handling, so the Bf 109 V23 third prototype was completed with detachable wingtips of semi-elliptical shape that restored all but 2.16sq ft (0.20sq m) of the previously deleted wing area, resulting in greatly enhanced handling. The Bf 109 V24 fourth prototype introduced a revised supercharger air inlet and a deeper oil cooler bath under the forward fuselage. From the beginning of the development programme it had been planned that the Bf 109F would switch to an armament scheme with the guns concentrated in the forward fuselage: thus the two 0.312in (7.92mm) MG 17 machine-guns with 500 rounds per gun were retained on the upper part of the nose, but the two 20mm MG FF cannon in the wing leading edges were replaced by a 15mm MG 151/15 cannon with 150 rounds in a moteur-canon installation firing through the hollow propeller shaft: the elimination of the wing-mounted guns certainly improved agility, and the loss of notional firepower was considered to be more than offset by the fact that the MG 151 was more reliable and faster-firing than the MG FF, and could be given a greater ammunition capacity as it was a belt-fed rather than drum-fed weapon.

As construction of the initial batch of Bf 109F-0 pre-production fighters was undertaken in the autumn of 1940, neither the DB 601E nor the MG 151 was ready for service, so these first aircraft were completed with a powerplant of one DB 601N engine rated at 1,200hp (895kW) for take-off and 1,270hp (947kW) at 16,405ft (5,000m), an armament of two MG 17 machine-guns and one 20mm MG FF/M cannon in the moteur-canon installation, and a normal take-off weight of 5,754lb (2,610kg). Evaluation of the Bf 109F-0 resulted in a mixed reception: all pilots were enthusiastic about the new fighter's improved performance and better combination of manoeuvrability and handling, but most were unhappy about the reduction in firepower. Even so, the advantages of the Bf 109F over the Bf 109E were very real and the full production of the type was authorised. The first model to emerge from this programme was the Bf 109F-1 that differed from the Bf 109F-0 in having a supercharger air inlet of round rather than square section. Production aircraft were available at the end of 1940, but full entry to service was delayed by the loss of several aircraft to a cause that was eventually discovered to have been the elimination of the tailplane bracing struts: lack of rigidity in the new tail unit allowed vibration that overlapped with engine vibration at certain r.p.m. to set up a sympathetic oscillation that resulted in structural failure. The problem was cured by the addition of external stiffener plates on the tail, and the Bf 109F-1 then entered service in February 1941.

Bf 109F-2: This was a development of the Bf 109F-1 with the 15mm MG 151 belt-fed cannon with 150 rounds in place of the 20mm MG FF/M drum-fed cannon and, as the first definitive variant of the 'Friedrich' series, this model was produced in a number of subvariants broadly analogous to those of the Bf 109E series with a power-boost system and/or tropicalisation features. The other details of the Bf 109F-2 included a powerplant of one DB 601N inverted-Vee piston engine rated at 1,200hp (895kW) for take-off and 1,270hp (947kW) at 16,405ft (5,000m); internal fuel capacity of 88 Imp gal (400 litres); external fuel capacity of up to 66 Imp gal (300 litres) in one drop tank; span of 32ft 6.5in (9.92m) with an aspect ratio of 6.11 and an area of 173.30sq ft (16.10sq m); length of 29ft 3.875in (8.94m); height of 8ft 6.33in (2.60m); empty weight of 5,188lb (2,353kg); normal take-off weight of 6,173lb (2,800kg); maximum take-off weight of 6,760lb (3,066kg); maximum level speed of 324kt (373mph; 600km/h) at 19,685ft (6,000m) declining to 279kt (321mph; 517km/h) at sea level; maximum cruising speed of 302kt (348mph; 560km/h) at 16,405ft (5,000m); economical cruising speed of 191kt (220mph; 354km/h) at sea level; maximum range of 475nm (547 miles; 880km) with drop tank; maximum rate of climb at sea level 3,860ft (1,177m) per minute; climb to 16,405ft (5,000m) in 5min 12sec, and service ceiling of 36,090ft (11,000m).

Bf 109F-3: This was basically the development of the Bf 109F-2 with the DB 601E engine that had originally been

Seen in the cockpit of his Messerschmitt Bf 109, Hauptmann Hans-Joachim Marseille was Germany leading ace in terms of Western Allied aircraft destroyed. Operating with the I Gruppe of Jagdgeschwader 27, Marseille shot down 158 Western Allied aircraft, 151 of them over North Africa.

planned for the Bf 109F series: the specific engine model was the DB 601E-1 rated at 1,350hp (1,007kW) for take-off and 1,300hp (969kW) at 18,045ft (5,500m).

Bf 109F-4: Produced in a parallel programme with the Bf 109F-3, this variant introduced the 20mm MG 151/20 version of the MG 151 cannon in the moteur-canon installation, this requiring a reduction in ammunition quantity from 200 to 150 rounds. The opportunity was also taken in this model to make a number of improvements, including better fuel tankage self-sealing capability, revised protection for the pilot in the form of the standard toughened glass windscreen and armour plate supplemented by additional toughened glass and armour plate for additional protection against lateral and stern attack, the Revi C/12D reflector gunsight, and a gun selector switch that allowed the cannon and machine-guns to be fired separately or collectively.

It was at this point that serious differences in opinion about the Bf 109F's armament arose: some Experten (aces) led by Werner Mölders favoured the current fit of one 20mm cannon and two 0.312in (7.92mm) machine-guns, while others led by Adolf Galland wanted a larger number of weapons so that average pilots stood a greater chance of scoring a decisive hit in fleeting engagements. A solution to these divergences of opinion was found in the evolution of

Although it had lost much of the Bf 109F's sophistication in terms of handling and was perhaps somewhat overpowered, the Messerschmitt Bf 109G was a highly successful fighter combining high performance with heavy and diverse armament.

a number of field conversion sets that allowed the creation of a number of different armament fits.

Bf 109F-5: This was the tactical reconnaissance fighter version of the Bf 109F-4 with the engine-mounted cannon removed, a single vertical camera added in the rear fuselage, and provision made for a 66 Imp gal (300 litre) ventral drop tank.

Bf 109F-6: This was a tactically more versatile derivative of the Bf 109F-5 with all armament removed and a special camera bay installed for the carriage of an Rb 20/30, Rb 50/30 or Rb 75/30 camera. Only a relatively small number of the Bf 109F-5 and Bf 109F-6 variants were produced, and by the end of 1941 the Bf 109F series had been replaced in production by the Bf 109G series.

Bf 109G-1: This 'Gustav' variant was numerically and operationally the most important model of the Bf 109 series to enter service in World War II and was a highly capable type that, with the aid of a number of kits, could be adapted for the full gamut of tactical fighter roles. Yet this capability was achieved only by the installation of an engine that many considered too powerful for the basic airframe, and this process resulted in handling characteristics that were decidedly inferior to those of the elegant but perhaps inadequately armed Bf 109F model. This was a penalty that the pilots of the Luftwaffe were generally happy to pay, after initial misgivings when the first Bf 109G fighters were issued to front-line squadrons early in 1942, because by mid-1941 it was becoming clear to an increasing number of German pilots that the Bf 109F's combination of excellent handling and adequate performance was not as important as the higher outright performance that could be achieved only at the cost of the poorer handling.

The Bf 109G was therefore planned from early 1941 as a development of the Bf 109F with a considerably more powerful engine and, in reflection of the fact that both cruising flight and combat were taking place at increasingly high altitudes, a pressurised cockpit. Evidence of the latter was discernible in the Bf 109G in the heavier framing of the cockpit and the elimination of the original type of quarterlight. The pressurisation system inevitably added to the weight of the basic airframe, and this escalation of weight was exacerbated by the need for structural strengthening to cope with the additional mass and power of the new engine. This additional weight also dictated the adoption of stronger and heavier main landing gear legs.

The engine selected for the new variant was the Daimler-Benz DB 605A inverted-Vee piston engine, which was a development of the DB 601E with bored-out cylinders for a greater swept capacity: the result was an engine with basically the same exterior dimensions as the DB 601E but with ratings of 1,475hp (1,100kW) for take-off and 1,355hp (1,010kW) at 18,700ft (5,700m). Accommodation of the new engine required a certain modification to the shape of the cowling, which now possessed an upper line of virtually constant contour between the spinner and the windscreen; the lower contour was changed by the need to fit a larger oil cooler. It was felt that there was no need for prototypes, so the first Bf 109G fighters were a small number of Bf 109G-0 pre-production fighters. The new DB 605A engine was not ready in time for these machines, which were built in the late summer of 1941, so they emerged with the DB 601E engine inherited from the Bf 109F. The same stricture did not apply to the Bf 109G-1 initial production model, which was delivered from the early spring of 1942 with a powerplant of one DB 605A-1 engine fitted as standard with the GM 1 nitrous oxide power-boost system. This added considerably to weight, the loaded weight being 7,055lb (3,200kg) with 25.3 Imp gal (115 litres) of liquid nitrous oxide weighing some 397lb (180kg), but use of the power-boost system yielded a major dividend in a power rating of 1,250hp (932kW) at an altitude of 27,890ft (8,500m).

The Bf 109G-1 was schemed as a pure fighter, and its fixed forward-firing armament was therefore restricted to one 20mm MG 151/20 cannon in a moteur-canon installation firing through the hollow propeller shaft and two 0.312in (7.92mm) MG 17 machine-guns on the upper part of the forward fuselage with synchronisation equipment to fire through the propeller disc. An armament change introduced in the tropicalised model was the replacement of the cannon by two 0.51in (13mm) MG 131 machine-guns with 300 rounds per gun: this alteration was prompted by the tendency of the cannon to jam when very hot, an occurrence that left the fighter with an armament of just two rifle-calibre machine-guns. The greater size of the heavy machine-guns now installed made it necessary to create bulged fairings on the fuselage over the gun breeches, and this led to the adoption of the nickname 'Beule' ('bump') for the Bf 109G-1/Trop.

Bf 109G-2: Produced in parallel with the Bf 109G-1 but entering service earlier as a result of its reduced complexity, the Bf 109G-2 differed from the Bf 109G-1 only in its lack of cockpit pressurisation. The variant could also be used in the reconnaissance role, with the MG 151/20 cannon removed and a single vertical camera installed in the rear fuselage.

Bf 109G-3: This was a version of the pressurised Bf 109G-1 with different radio equipment.

Bf 109G-4: This was a version of the unpressurised Bf 109G-2 with different radio equipment, and could also be used in the reconnaissance role with the MG 151/20 cannon removed and a single vertical camera installed in the rear fuselage.

These initial four variants of the Bf 109G series were produced almost simultaneously, and first entered service in April 1942 with JG 2 and JG 26 that were located at bases to the south of the English Channel. The RAF first encountered the Bf 109G in May 1942, and soon discovered that the type was a formidable opponent whose capabilities were diminished only by its indifferent armament.

Bf 109G-5: Although the first subvariants of the Bf 109G series proved more than adequate for the fighter tasks demanded of them, there was dissatisfaction with the GM 1 nitrous oxide power-boost system which, it was felt, was less effective than a more capable supercharging system. Fitted with a machine-gun armament of two 0.51in (13mm) MG 131 weapons, like all subsequent Bf 109G variants, the Bf 109G-5 had the pressurised cockpit and was powered by the DB 605AS engine that used the larger supercharger developed for the DB 603. The greater width and height of the supercharger resulted in a somewhat clumsy exterior inlet arrangement that was retained for all later members of the Bf 109G series. The improved supercharging system was responsible for the DB 605AS engine's rating of 1,200hp (895kW) at 26,245ft (8,000m).

Bf 109G-6: Delivered from the autumn of 1942, the Bf 109G-6 lacked the pressurised cockpit (as did all later Bf 109G variants), introduced a moteur-canon installation of one 30mm MK 108 cannon with 60 rounds, had full provision for R͵sts‰tze, was able to accommodate several variants of the DB 605A engine (or, from early 1944, the DB 605A engine), and had a 25.3 Imp gal (115 litre) insulated tank for nitrous oxide or a methanol/water mixture so that either the GM 1 or MW 50 power-boost systems could be used. The DB 603AM engine with the MW 50 system had a normal take-off power of 1,475hp (1,100kW) that could be boosted to 1,800hp (1,342kW), and the boost system increased the power available at 13,450ft (4,100m) to 1,700hp (1,268kW).

Bf 109G-8: It was planned in the early part of 1943 to standardise a variant of the Bf 109G-6 with the U2 and U4 modifications, but this scheme was impractical as a result of the thoroughly dispersed nature of Bf 109 production, so the type was overtaken by the Bf 109G-8 that was built in small numbers as a specialised reconnaissance derivative of the Bf 109G-6. The Bf 109G-8 was powered by either the DB 603A-1 or DB 603AS engine, the gun armament was confined to one 30mm MK 108 cannon that was sometimes replaced by a 20mm MG 151/20 cannon, and the reconnaissance capability was provided by an Rb 12.7/7 or Rb 32/7 camera in the rear fuselage.

Bf 109G-10: This was the result of a major effort to standardise a single model that could then be built in very

The Mistel (mistletoe) concept combined a Junkers Ju 88 high-speed bomber, with its crew replaced by a huge explosive charge, controlled by a fighter (in this instance a Messerschmitt Bf 109G) mounted on struts above it. Once the pilot in the fighter had set the bomber on its final trajectory to the target, normally a bridge or other such major unit, he released his fighter and departed, leaving the bomber to impact with the target and blow up.

large numbers. Introduced to production in the spring of 1944, the Bf 109G-10 was basically the Bf 109G-6 with the revised powerplant of one DB 605D engine with the MW 50 methanol/water power-boost system for ratings of 1,850hp (1,379kW) for take-off and 1,600hp (1,193kW) at 19,685ft (6,000m). The Bf 109G-10 carried a fixed forward-firing armament of one engine-mounted cannon in the form of one 30mm MK 108 with 60 rounds or one 20mm MG 151/20 with 150 rounds, and two fuselage-mounted machine-guns in the form of 0.51in (13mm) MG 131 weapons with 300 rounds per gun; these were used with the Revi 16/B reflector sight. The Bf 109G-10 also had provision for a 66 Imp gal (300 litre) ventral drop tank.

The Bf 109G-10 with the DB 605DC engine was the fastest of all Bf 109 variants, its maximum level speed in 'clean' condition at a weight of 6,834lb (3,100kg) being 370kt (426mph; 686km/h) at 24,280ft (7,400m) declining to 297kt (342mph; 550km/h) at sea level; the climb rate was also excellent, an altitude of 19,685ft (6,000m) being reached in 5min 48sec. Fortunately for the Allies, however, the Bf 109G-10 was seldom encountered in 'clean' condition, for virtually every such fighter was fitted with a R,stsatz on entry to service.

Bf 109G-12: This was the tandem two-seat conversion trainer member of the Bf 109G series.

Bf 109G-14: Although it had been decided in 1944 to concentrate on the standardised Bf 109K model, the interim period was occupied by construction of the Bf 109G-14 that entered service in the late summer of 1944. This was basically the Bf 109G-10 with the DB 605AM engine, the bulged so-called 'Galland hood', an armament of one 20mm MG 151/20 cannon and two 0.51in (13mm) MG 131 machine-guns, and a fixed tailwheel.

Bf 109G-16: This final version of the Bf 109G series was a development of the Bf 109G-14, with the DB 605D engine, armour protection for the oil cooler and coolant radiators, and the R1 and R6 R‚sts‰tze installed on the production line as permanent fixtures. More than 1,500 Bf 109G fighters were completed in 1945 before Germany's surrender to the Allies.

The Bf 109H was a planned high-altitude model with the DB 605B engine rated at 1,600hp (1,193kW) for take-off, the wing enlarged to a span of 43ft 6in (13.25m) with an aspect ratio of 8.02 and an area of 235.73sq ft (21.90sq m), and an armament of one 30mm MK 108 engine-mounted cannon and two 20mm MG 151/20 wing-mounted cannon with 60 and 200 rounds per gun respectively.

Bf 109K-2: The Bf 109K series was planned as a standardised type that could be built more rapidly than the plethora of variants and subvariants that had characterised the Bf 109G series. The type was based on the airframe of the Bf 109G-10 with the 'Galland hood', and included as standard some of the progressive changes that had been introduced in that subvariant as Umr‚st-Baus‰tze (factory conversion sets) together with a number of aerodynamic improvements that were individually small but collectively significant. The first Bf 109K-0 pre-production aircraft appeared in September 1944 to a basic design that differed from that of the Bf 109G-10 most noticeably in the raised line of its cowling, longer spinner for the propeller, a larger inset rudder tab supplemented by a large trailing tab, replacement of the two fuselage-mounted 0.51in (13mm) MG 131 machine-guns by two 15mm MG 151 cannon to supplement the engine-mounted 30mm MK 108 cannon as the fixed forward-firing battery, and a powerplant of one DB 605DB inverted-Vee piston engine with the GM 1 nitrous oxide power-boost system. Operational trials with these pre-production aircraft revealed no major deficiencies, so the type was authorised for production as the Bf 109K-2 with a powerplant of either one DB 605ASCM engine or one DB 605DCM engine with the GM 1 power-boost system.

Bf 109K-4: In its original form, this differed from the Bf 109K-2 only in having a pressurised cockpit, but later examples were revised with the 30mm MK 103 cannon in place of the MK 108 weapon of the same calibre in the moteur-canon installation.

The details of the Bf 109K-4 included an armament of one 30mm MK 103 or MK 108 fixed forward-firing cannon with 60 rounds in a moteur-canon installation and two 15mm MG 151/15 fixed forward-firing cannon with 220 rounds per gun in the upper part of the forward fuselage with synchronisation equipment to fire through the propeller disc, and up to 551lb (250kg) of disposable stores carried on one hardpoint under the fuselage; powerplant of one DB 605ASCM inverted-Vee piston engine rated at

2,000hp (1,491kW) for take-off and 1,800hp (1,342kW) at 16,405ft (5,000m); internal fuel capacity of 88 Imp gal (400 litres); external fuel capacity of up to 66 Imp gal (300 litres) in one drop tank; span of 32ft 8.5in (9.97m) with an aspect ratio of 6.17 and an area of 173.30sq ft (16.10sq m); length of 29ft 0.5in (8.85m); height of 8ft 2.5in (2.50m); empty weight of 5,247lb (2,380kg); normal take-off weight of 7,440lb (3,375kg); maximum take-off weight of 7,937lb (3,600kg); maximum level speed of 378kt (435mph; 700km/h) at 24,610ft (7,500m) declining to 328kt (378mph; 608km/h) at sea level; typical range of 309nm (356 miles; 573km); maximum rate of climb at sea level of 4,820ft (1,469m) per minute; climb to 16,405ft (5,000m) in 3min 0sec, and service ceiling of 41,010ft (12,500m).

BF 109K-6: This was the heavy fighter version of the Bf 109K-4 intended for the anti-bomber role with an armament of one 30mm MK 103 cannon in the moteur-canon installation, two 0.51in (13mm) MG 131 machine-guns in the upper part of the forward fuselage, and two 30mm MK 103 cannon in underwing gondolas. The Bf 109K-6 had a maximum take-off weight of 7,925lb (3,595kg) and was distinctly unwieldy in the air, so it is perhaps fortunate for German fighter pilots that relatively few of the type were delivered after its service debut in January 1945.

Bf 109K-14: Delivered only in very small numbers during the last two weeks before Germany's surrender at the end of World War II in Europe, the Bf 109K-14 was the ultimate version of the Bf 109 series, and was characterised by its use of the DB 605L engine with a two-stage supercharger and the MW 50 methanol/water power-boost system: the engine delivered 1,700hp (1,268kW) for take-off and 1,350hp (1,007kW) at 31,400ft (9,570m), and the capabilities of this engine allowed the Bf 109K-14 to attain the same maximum level speed as the Bf 109K-4 but at an altitude of 37,730ft (11,500m) rather than 19,685ft (6,000m). The fixed forward-firing armament of the Bf 109K-14 was somewhat lighter than that of the Bf 109K-4, however, and comprised one 30mm cannon (either the MK 103 or MK 108) in the moteur-canon installation and two 0.51in (13mm) MG 131 machine-guns in the upper part of the forward fuselage.

Nakajima Ki-43 Hayabusa 'Oscar'

Manufacturer: Nakajima Hikoki K.K.

Country of origin: Japan

Specification: Ki-43-IIb Hayabusa

Type: Fighter and fighter-bomber

Accommodation: Pilot in an enclosed cockpit

Entered service: Autumn 1941

Left service: Late 1940s

Operational equipment: Standard communication and navigation equipment, plus a reflector gunsight

Armament: Two 0.5in (12.7mm) Ho-103 (Type 1) fixed forward-firing machine-guns with 250 rounds per gun in the upper part of the forward fuselage with synchronisation equipment to fire through the propeller disc, and up to 1,102lb (500kg) of disposable stores carried on two hardpoints (both under the wings with each unit rated at 551lb/250kg), and generally comprising two 551 or 132lb (250 or 60kg) bombs

Powerplant: One Nakajima Ha-115 (Army Type 1) radial piston engine rated at 1,150hp (857kW) for take-off and 980hp (731kW) at 18,735ft (5,710m)

Fuel capacity: Internal fuel 119.9 Imp gal (545 litres); external fuel up to 88 Imp gal (400 litres) in two drop tanks

Dimensions: Span 35ft 6.75in (10.84m); aspect ratio 5.49; area 230.37sq ft (21.40sq m); length 29ft 3.25in (8.92m); height 10ft 8.75in (3.27m)

Weights: Empty 4,211lb (1,910kg) equipped; normal take-off 5,710lb (2,590kg); maximum take-off 6,450lb (2,926kg)

Performance: Maximum level speed 'clean' 286kt (330mph; 531km/h) at 13,125ft (4,000m); cruising speed 237kt (273mph; 439km/h) at optimum altitude; maximum range 1,727nm (1,988 miles; 3,200km) with drop tanks; typical range 950nm (1,094 miles; 1,760km) with internal fuel; climb to 16,405ft (5,000m) in 5min 49sec; service ceiling 36,750ft (11,200m)

Variants

Ki-43-I Hayabusa: Known to the Imperial Japanese army air force as the Hayabusa (peregrine falcon) and to the Allies by the reporting name 'Oscar', this was the most advanced fighter available to the Imperial Japanese army air force in the opening phases of the Pacific War (1941-45). The type came as a considerable shock to the Allied air forces, which had deployed into these regions only the more obsolescent of its 'modern' monoplane fighters in the belief, apparently confirmed by intelligence data, that the Imperial Japanese army air force had not yet fielded a monoplane fighter with retractable landing gear to replace the Nakajima Ki-27 with its fixed landing gear. The Ki-43 was encountered in large numbers over China, and in smaller but nonetheless significant numbers over the Philippines, Malaya, Burma, the Netherlands East Indies and New Guinea. In all these theatres the type proved to have the measure of Allied fighters in terms of agility and overall performance, but also revealed its lack of offensive firepower together with a lightweight and basically unprotected airframe that was incapable of absorbing much battle damage.

The origins of the type can be traced to 1937, when the Imperial Japanese army air force started the process of acquiring a successor to the Ki-27. In a break with its previous practice, the service decided not to proceed via the competitive design process, but in December 1937 issued to Nakajima the requirement for an advanced monoplane fighter providing agility at least equal to that of the Ki-27 and with the same armament of two 0.303in (7.7mm) machine-guns, and also possessing markedly improved performance that included a maximum level speed of 270kt (311mph; 500km/h) at optimum altitude, range of 432nm (497 miles; 800km), and climb to 16,405ft (5,000m) in 5 minutes. Nakajima entrusted the task of designing the new fighter to a team under the supervision of Hideo Itokawa, and this team quickly evolved a cantilever low-wing monoplane of basically all-metal construction with fabric-covered control surfaces.

Construction of the three prototypes proceeded rapidly, and the first prototype made its maiden flight in December 1938 wit8nm (746 miles; 1,200km) with drop tanks; climb to 16,405ft (5,000m) in 5min 30sec, and service ceiling of 38,500ft (11,735m). Production of the Ki-43-I series, all delivered by Nakajima between April 1941 and February 1943, totalled 716 aircraft.

The Ki-43-I soon acquired an excellent reputation within the Imperial Japanese army air force, and the reluctant admiration of its enemies, who found themselves seldom able to keep this agile air-combat fighter in their sights for more than a few moments. The Achilles' heel of the Ki-43-I, as with most Japanese warplanes of this period early in the Pacific War, was its combination of a very light structure and lack of any protection for the pilot or for the fuel supply. Allied pilots therefore found that even a short burst was sufficient to cause a structural failure, kill or wound the pilot, or set fire to the fuel supply.

The Allies' lack of co-ordination meant that the type initially received two reporting names: in the CBI (China, Burma and India) theatre the Ki-43 was thought to be a development of the Ki-27 with retractable main landing gear units and was allocated the name 'Jim'; while in the South-West Pacific Area the name 'Oscar' was given and then adopted universally after it had been appreciated that the Ki-43 was not a Ki-27 derivative.

Ki-43-II Hayabusa: From the beginning of the Ki-43

programme it had been planned that a more powerful engine would eventually be fitted, and soon after the Ki-43-I had entered service, five aircraft were modified with the Nakajima Ha-115 (Army Type 1) radial piston engine rated at 1,150hp (857kW) for take-off and 980hp (731kW) at 18,735ft (5,710m) and driving a three-blade metal propeller of the constant-speed type. Completed between February and May 1942, these prototypes were followed by three pre-production aircraft constructed between June and August 1942 and, from November 1942, by the Ki-43-IIa production model that entered service with the designation Army Type 1 Fighter Model 2A Hayabusa.

The Ki-43-II series differed from the Ki-43-I series in a number of respects other than the powerplant, most notably the relocation of the supercharger air inlet from its original position under the cowling to a new position on the upper part of the cowling lip, the reduction in wing span and area for improved speed at low and medium altitudes, a slight heightening of the windscreen and cockpit canopy, the introduction of a new reflector gunsight, the revision of the underwing hardpoints for the carriage of 551lb (250kg) bombs as alternatives to drop tanks, and a measure of protection in the form of armour plate for the pilot and self-sealing for the fuel tanks.

Production of the Ki-43-IIa was comparatively short-lived, for the type was soon supplanted by the Ki-43-IIb (Army Type 1 Fighter Model 2B Hayabusa) that in its first form was distinguishable only by changes to the carburettor air inlet, which up to this time had been located under the cowling but was now incorporated within the oil cooler that was changed from an annular type (located around the propeller shaft to the rear of the spinner) to a honeycomb unit under the engine cowling. Later changes in the Ki-43-IIb production standard included a relocation of the hardpoints to positions farther outboard under the wings to prevent bombs from hitting the propeller in dive-bombing attacks, and the movement of the carburettor inlet/oil cooler installation to a position farther to the rear. All these changes were standardised in the Ki-43-II Kai, which also introduced individual ejector exhausts (for a measure of additional thrust) in place of the earlier collector ring arrangement. The model also introduced a number of airframe modifications designed to facilitate production and simplify field maintenance.

With a number of major commitments to the Imperial

Japanese navy air force as well as the Imperial Japanese army air force, Nakajima was unable to satisfy demand for the Ki-43 series, and the Imperial Japanese army air force therefore brought two other manufacturing sources into the Hayabusa programme. These were the Dai-Ichi Rikugun Kokusho (1st Army Air Arsenal) and Tachikawa Hikoki K.K., both located at Tachikawa. The army facility soon showed that it lacked the skills requirement for mass production of a fighter and was pulled out of the programme after delivering 49 examples of the Ki-43-IIa from Nakajima-supplied components, but Tachikawa proved to be more successful and between May 1943 and August 1945 delivered 2,629 aircraft of various Hayabusa models to supplement Nakajima's total of 3,208 aircraft (716 Ki-43-I and 2,492 Ki-43-II fighters).

Ki-43-III Hayabusa: This was the main variant produced by Tachikawa, after Nakajima had delivered 10 prototype aircraft between May and August 1944. The Ki-43-III was basically a development of the Ki-43-II Kai with the uprated powerplant of one Nakajima Ha-115-II engine rated at 1,190hp (887kW) for take-off and 950hp (708kW) at 20,340ft (6,200m). The improved fighter entered service as the Army Type 1 Fighter Model 3A Hayabusa, and was dimensionally identical to the Ki-43-IIb. In respects other than its engine, the Ki-43-IIIa differed from the Ki-43-IIb in details such as its internal fuel capacity of 144 Imp gal (655 litres) that could be supplemented by 92.4 Imp gal (420 litres) carried in two drop tanks; empty weight of 4,233lb (1,920kg); normal take-off weight of 5,644lb (2,560kg); maximum take-off weight of 6,746lb (3,060kg); maximum level speed of 311kt (358mph; 576km/h) at 21,920ft (6,680m); cruising speed of 239kt (275mph; 442km/h) at 8,200ft (2,500m); maximum range of 1,727nm (1,990 miles; 3,202km) with drop tanks; standard range of 1,144nm (1,317 miles; 2,120km) with internal fuel; climb to 16,405ft (5,000m) in 5min 19sec, and service ceiling of 37,400ft (11,400m).

The Ki-43-I was also operated in small numbers by the Thai air force during the Pacific War, and after the war the Ki-43 was also flown in small numbers by the air arm of the nationalist forces fighting a return of Dutch imperial power to the Netherlands East Indies (now Indonesia), and by the French fighting the communist guerrilla forces in French Indo-China.

Republic P-47 Thunderbolt

Manufacturer: Republic Aviation Corporation

Country of origin: USA

Specification: P-47D-22 Thunderbolt

Type: Fighter and fighter-bomber

Accommodation: Pilot in an enclosed cockpit

Entered service: Mid-1942

Left service: 1960s

Operational equipment: Standard communication and navigation equipment, plus a reflector gunsight

Armament: Eight 0.5in (12.7mm) Browning MG53-2 fixed forward-firing machine-guns with a maximum of 425 rounds but normal 267 rounds per gun in the wing leading edges, and up to 2,500lb (1,134kg) of disposable stores carried on three hardpoints (one under the fuselage rated at 500lb/227kg and two under the wings with each unit rated at 1,000lb/454kg), and generally comprising two 1,000lb (454kg) bombs or three 500lb (227kg) bombs, or up to ten 5in (127mm) HVAR air-to-surface rockets

The P-47N was the variant of the Republic P-47 Thunderbolt fighter and fighter-bomber optimised for long-range operations over the Pacific, and therefore had a longer-span wing and considerable enlarged internal fuel capacity.

Powerplant: One Pratt & Whitney R-2800-59 radial piston engine rated at 2,000hp (1,491kW) for take-off and 2,000hp (1,491kW) at 33,000ft (10,060m)

Fuel capacity: Internal fuel 254 Imp gal (1,154.5 litres); external fuel up to 383 Imp gal (1,471.3 litres) in three drop tanks

Dimensions: Span 40ft 9in (12.42m); aspect ratio 5.535; area 300.00sq ft (27.87sq m); length 36ft 1in (10.99m); height 14ft 7in (4.44m); wheel track 15ft 7in (4.75m)

Weights: Empty 10,700lb (4,853kg) equipped; normal take-off 13,500lb (6,124kg); maximum take-off 16,200lb (7,348kg)

Performance: Maximum level speed 'clean' 378kt (435mph; 700km/h) at 30,000ft (9,145m) declining to 311kt (358mph; 576km/h) at 5,000ft (1,525m); cruising speed 304kt (350mph; 563km/h) at optimum altitude; maximum range 1,498nm (1,725 miles; 2,776km) with drop tanks; typical range 686nm (790 miles; 1,271km) with internal fuel; maximum rate of climb at 5,000ft (1,524m) of 3,100ft (945m) per minute; climb to 15,000ft (4,570m) in 5min 36sec; service ceiling 42,000ft (12,800m)

Variants
P-47B Thunderbolt: The Thunderbolt was one of the classic warplanes of World War II, and remains an enduring example of the fashion in which the Americans can 'think big'

and produce an item that is visually impressive yet packed with capability as a result of the careful combination of high power and clean design. Everything about the 'Jug' was on a large scale, and in the course of 545,575 operational sorties, by a total of 15,683 aircraft completed up to August 1945 and flown in every US theatre but Alaska, the fighter claimed the destruction of 7,067 enemy aircraft (including 3,72 in the air) for the loss of 3,499 of its own number (including 824 in the air, for a 'kill/loss' ratio of 4.6/1). The P-47 also operated with increasing success in the fighter-bomber role, and in this task claimed the destruction of 9,000 locomotives, 86,000 railroad cars, 6,000 armoured vehicles, 68,000 motor vehicles, and 60,000 horse-drawn vehicles.

The origins of the P-47 can be traced to an earlier form of the Republic Aviation Corporation, namely the Seversky Aircraft Corporation created in 1931 by Alexander P. de Seversky, an expatriate Russian. This organisation built a number of types before its chief designer, Alexander Kartveli, evolved the P-35 fighter that was the production version of the SEV-1XP prototype that was itself the SEV-2XP two-seat prototype revised with single-seat accommodation and retractable landing gear. This type established the type of fighter for which Kartveli became celebrated, for it was a comparatively large cantilever low-wing monoplane of basically all-metal construction with a wing of semi-elliptical planform and a corpulent fuselage carrying a powerful radial piston engine.

In 1938 the Seversky Aircraft Corporation ran into financial difficulties and was reorganised. During the first part of 1939 Seversky himself left the company, and in June the Seversky Aircraft Corporation was renamed as the Republic Aviation Corporation. Kartveli continued as chief engineer, and during this period he was considering how to evolve a thoroughly modern fighter offering the highest possible performance through development of the Seversky/Republic design philosophy: this emphasised the use of a powerful radial piston engine and a massive airframe of considerable strength. Kartveli's conclusion was that good performance could only be achieved by the use of the most powerful radial engine in a very clean airframe, and with an engine installation of very low drag. Evidence of this philosophy was found in the US Army Air Corps (USAAC) 1939 fighter competition, in which Republic entered two prototypes. The less advanced of the two was the AP-2 (USAAC designation XP-41) that was the P-35 revised with internal inward-retracting (rather than external rearward-retracting) main landing gear units and a powerplant of one Pratt & Whitney R-1830-19 radial engine rated at 1,200hp (895kW) for take-off, while the more advanced was the AP-4 that was basically the AP-2 with an engine boosted by a turbocharger installed in the central fuselage and drawing its air through an inlet in the port wing root.

The USAAC was not particularly enthusiastic about the AP-4, and the competition was won by the Curtiss Model 81 that was ordered into production as the P-40. Even so, the service was sufficiently impressed with the technical advance represented by the AP-4 to order a batch of 13 YP-43 Lancer service test aircraft, with the R-1830-35 radial engine rated at 1,200hp (895kW) for take-off and using a turbocharger installation revised with its inlet in the engine cowling. The YP-43 aircraft paved the way for a small number of production aircraft, namely 54 examples of the P-43 Lancer with the R-1830-47 engine rated at 1,200hp (895kW) for take-off, and 205 examples of the P-43A Lancer with the R-1830-49 radial engine with the same rating.

As these aircraft were being developed and built, Kartveli was considering how to optimise the AP-4's design philosophy. The key to further improved performance, as Kartveli already knew, was the use of either a considerably more powerful radial engine in a large airframe, or a Vee piston engine of more modest power in a smaller and less 'draggy' airframe. Most of Kartveli's contemporaries in the design of land-based fighters for the USAAC had chosen the Vee-engined option: Bell had adopted a Vee engine buried in the central fuselage for its P-39, Curtiss had changed from the radial to the Vee engine in extrapolating the P-40 from the P-36, and Lockheed had selected a powerplant of two Vee piston engines for its radical P-38 fighter with a twin-boom layout.

Kartveli was still attracted by the merit of the higher-power radial engine, however, although he conceded that a very carefully planned engine installation would be required to mitigate the inherently higher drag of such a powerplant. Republic therefore moved forward to consideration of developments of the P-43 Lancer. Via a convoluted process of successive design evolutions and both prototype and production orders, this led to the September 1940 decision for the cancellation of Republic's other prototypes so that it could concentrate on the most promising of them, namely the XP-47B with a high-rated powerplant based on a potent

In the ground-attack role, the Republic P-47 Thunderbolt assumed the mantle of the first-generation monoplane fighter-bombers such as the Curtiss P-40E with a wing-mounted armament of six 0.5in (12.7mm) Browning machine guns.

radial engine with excellent high-altitude capability through the incorporation of a turbocharger. The crux of the turbocharger installation was that the additional power it provided would have to be significantly greater than its weight and drag penalties.

Kartveli decided that the need to optimise the turbocharger installation demanded a complete revision of the fuselage to ensure an even balance of the engine and turbocharger masses, and also the correct shaping of the ducts supplying air to the turbocharger, compressed air from the turbocharger to the engine, and exhaust gases from the engine to the turbocharger, whose blower was powered by a turbine driven by these gases before they were exhausted. Thus the turbocharger was installed in the rear fuselage, some 22ft (6.7m) to the rear of the propeller. Exhaust gases were collected by two exhaust rings, one each for the left- and right-hand groups of cylinders, and then channelled along two ducts, one on each side of the lower fuselage, to power the turbine before being exhausted through a ventral opening close to the tail. Air for the blower was collected from an inlet in the cowling under the engine, a position in which the ram effect was boosted by the propeller, and then ducted along the bottom of the fuselage towards the turbocharger. Before reaching this point, however, the air was divided: some of it was directed into the blower for compression, and some of it was used in the intercooler for temperature-control purposes before being dumped via electrically controlled doors in the sides of the fuselage just forward of the turbocharger itself. Finally, the air compressed in the turbocharger and then lowered in temperature by the intercooler was directed along the sides of the fuselage in two ducts to the engine carburettors.

It was around this complete powerplant installation (engine, turbocharger, intercooler and associated ducting) that Kartveli planned the fuselage as a very substantial unit of light alloy semi-monocoque construction. The tail unit was of the plain type, and the cantilever mid/low-set wing was of semi-elliptical planform with dihedral, taper in thickness and chord, and the standard trailing-edge combination of outboard Frise-type ailerons and inboard slotted flaps; dive-recovery brakes were fitted under the inner wing panels ahead of the flaps. The airframe was completed by the landing gear, which was of the fully retractable tailwheel type with wide-track main units.

The XP-47B made its maiden flight in May 1941, with a powerplant of one XR-2800-21 radial engine rated at a nominal 2,000hp (1,491kW) at 27,800ft (8,475m) but in fact delivering less than this because of a number of factors including poor sealing of the turbocharger ducts: for its time, the XP-47B was the largest and heaviest fighter planned for the USAAC, which one month later became the US Army Air Forces (USAAF). The XP-47B soon proved itself an invaluable development tool, and Republic completed the first of an eventual 170 P-47B production aircraft in March 1942. This differed from the XP-47B mainly in having the R-2800-21 radial engine, a rearward-sliding canopy section, metal- rather than fabric-covered control surfaces, and a number of internal changes.

The other details of the P-47B included an armament of eight 0.5in (12.7mm) Browning machine-guns with 267 rounds per gun; span of 40ft 9.25in (12.41m) with an aspect ratio of 5.54 and an area of 300.00sq ft (91.44sq m); length of 35ft 5.25in (10.80m); height of 14ft 1.75in (4.31m); empty weight of 9,346lb (4,239kg); normal take-off weight of 12,245lb (5,554kg); maximum take-off weight of 13,360lb (6,060kg); maximum level speed of 372kt (429mph; 690km/h) at 27,000ft (8,230m) declining to 295kt (340mph; 547km/h) at 5,000ft (1,524m); cruising speed of 291kt (335mph; 539km/h) at 10,000ft (3,048m); typical range of 478nm (550 miles; 885km); initial climb rate of 2,560ft

(780m) per minute; climb to 15,000ft (4,570m) in 6min 42sec, and service ceiling of 42,000ft (12,800m).

All 170 P-47B Thunderbolt fighters were completed and delivered within a period of six months, but saw no operational service. The type was retained in the United States, mainly for use by the 56th Fighter Group for the training of pilots who would eventually fight overseas with later variants of the Thunderbolt.

P-47C Thunderbolt: Delivered from September 1942 to the extent of 602 aircraft, this was the first fully operational variant of the Thunderbolt series. The P-47C was powered by the R-2800-59 version of the Double Wasp radial engine, rated at 2,300hp (1,715kW) at 27,000ft (8,230m) with the aid of a water-injection system whose tank required a lengthening of the fuselage to 36ft 1.25in (11.00m). This change also made it possible to add a centreline hardpoint for the carriage of a drop tank. The main visual identification of the P-47C, apart from the longer forward fuselage, was the replacement of the P-47B's forward-raked radio mast by a vertical mast in the same position above and behind the cockpit. In other respects, the P-47C differed from the P-47D in details such as its empty weight of 9,900lb (4,491kg); normal take-off weight of 13,500lb (6,124kg); maximum take-off weight of 14,925lb (6,770kg); maximum level speed of 376kt (433mph; 697km/h) at 30,000ft (9,145m) declining to 306kt (353mph; 568km/h) at 5,000ft (1,524m); maximum cruising speed of 304kt (350mph; 563km/h) at 10,000ft (3,048m); economical cruising speed of 201kt (231mph; 372km/h) at 10,000ft (3,048m); maximum range of 1,085.5nm (1,250 miles; 2,012km) with drop tank; typical range of 556nm (640 miles; 1,030km) with internal fuel; initial climb rate of 2,780ft (847m) per minute; climb to 15,000ft (4,570m) in 7min 12sec, and service ceiling of 42,000ft (12,800m).

P-47D Thunderbolt: Shortly before the P-47C entered combat for the first time in April 1943, Republic started deliveries of an improved model that had been ordered in October 1941. This initial order had covered 850 aircraft to be built at Republic's original facility at Farmingdale in New York, and at much the same time the USAAF had placed supplementary orders for similar aircraft to be built by Republic, at a new government-owned facility at Evansville in Indiana, and by Curtiss at its facility at Buffalo in New

The Republic P-47D Thunderbolt was initially built with the original type of cockpit with a raised turtledeck behind it, but in its definitive form gained this type of bubble canopy and cut-down rear fuselage for much superior fields of vision.

York. Both Evansville and Buffalo delivered their first P-47s in December 1942, and such was the pace of production that for each P-47 delivered in 1942, eight were delivered in 1943 and thirteen in 1944. Virtually all these aircraft were P-47D models built by the two Republic production facilities, or the similar P-47G from the Curtiss production facility.

In its initial forms, up to and including the P-47D-20-RE and P-47D-23-RA blocks from Farmingdale and Evansville respectively, the P-47D was virtually indistinguishable from the later-production P-47C. The only major changes in the P-47D were a propeller with a diameter of 12ft 2in (3.71m), a redesigned turbocharger exhaust system with an adjustable duct, redesigned vents for the engine accessories, two additional sections of cooling gills on the rear of the engine section on each side, additional armour protection for the pilot, and an increase in the maximum ammunition capacity from 267 to 425 rounds per gun. As production of the P-47D continued during 1943, the type's escort role was gradually assumed by the North American P-51 Mustang with its somewhat better range capability, and the P-47D was freed for other tasks. It was at this stage that the type began to mature in its definitive form as a truly formidable fighter-bomber. In this task the ventral hardpoint was adapted from the P-47D-6-RE and P-47D-11-RA blocks for the carriage of a 500lb (227kg) bomb in place of the drop tank.

This adaptation curtailed range, so the next step was the restoration of external fuel capacity by the addition of extra hardpoints, which was achieved in the P-47D-15-RE and P-47D-15-RA blocks onward by the incorporation of two underwing hardpoints. These were each able to carry one

124.9 Imp gal (567.8 litre) drop tank or alternatively two 1,000 or 500lb (454 or 227kg) bombs. This allowed the P-47D to carry a maximum short-range disposable load of 2,500lb (1,134kg), but weight considerations meant that the carriage of the maximum external warload had to be balanced by a reduction in machine-gun ammunition capacity to the original figure of 267 rounds per gun. Finally, from the P-47D-35-RA block the Thunderbolt was delivered with provision for zero-length underwing rocket launchers: these totalled five on each side (only three if bombs or drop tanks were carried), and could each carry one 5in (127mm) HVAR air-to-surface rocket.

The P47D production development programme amounted to 6,510 Farmingdale-built and 6,093 Evansville-built aircraft, for a total of 12,603 P-47D warplanes. Other developments were designed to improve the P-47D's combat efficiency: the P-47D-25-RE and P-47D-26-RA blocks had internal fuel capacity increased to 308.1 Imp gal (1,400.6 litres), and they also featured a clear-view 'bubble' canopy with a fixed forward section and a rearward-sliding rear section (which eliminated the previous 'razorback' fairing that extended rearward from the canopy), that gave the pilot a full 360-degree field of vision. The reduction in keel area adversely affected directional stability, however, so from the P-47D-26-RE and P-47D-30-RA blocks, a small dorsal fin was added as a forward extension of the fixed fin. Finally, measures were taken to improve the performance of the P-47D, especially in climb, at the lower altitudes at which it now almost invariably operated: the P-47D-22-RE introduced a Hamilton Standard metal propeller of 13ft 0in (3.96m) diameter with four wider-chord 'paddle' blades, and the P-47D-23-RA introduced a similar Curtiss Electric propeller.

A number of P-47Ds were supplied to the USSR (203 aircraft) and also to allies such as Brazil (50 aircraft), France (446 aircraft), Mexico and Britain (240 with the original framed canopy for service with the local designation Thunderbolt Mk I, and 590 with the 'bubble' canopy for service with the local designation Thunderbolt Mk II). Many of the aircraft were also supplied to friendly nations after the end of World War II.

The next two variants were experimental models, and comprised the XP-47E and XP-47F. The XP-47E designation was applied to the last P-47B airframe that was completed in 1943 with a pressurised cockpit, and the XP-47F designation was applied to a single P-47B that was converted for trials with a laminar-flow wing.

P-47G Thunderbolt: This was the Curtiss-built version of the Thunderbolt, and 354 were completed with the original type of framed canopy and rear-fuselage 'razorback' fairing. The first 60 aircraft were completed to a P-47C standard, while 294 were to the P-47D standard, the final 234 of them with the ventral hardpoint for the carriage of a bomb or drop tank.

Next in designation sequence came a number of experimental models. The two XP-47H aircraft were P-47D conversions with the powerplant of one Chrysler XI-2220-1 inverted-Vee piston engine, with a maximum rating of 2,500hp (1,864kW) and installed in a finely tapered nose that increased overall length to 38ft 4in (11.68m). The XP-47J was a single P-47D conversion with the armament reduced to six 0.5in (12.7mm) machine-guns and the powerplant changed to one R-2800-57(C) radial engine with a maximum rating of 2,800hp (2,088kW) with the aid of a revised turbocharger installation using a separate air inlet. In August 1944, this conversion became the first piston-engined aeroplane in the world to achieve a maximum level speed in excess of 435kt (500mph; 805km/h) when it reached 438.5kt (505mph; 813km/h) at 34,450ft (10,500m). The XP-47K was a P-47D airframe used for the development of the 'bubble' canopy, and the XP-47L was another P-47D conversion used to test the increased internal fuel capacity adopted in late-production P-47Ds.

P-47M Thunderbolt: When the Germans first launched the Fieseler Fi 103 (or V-1) flying bomb at southern Britain in June 1944, the USAAF decided to procure a 'sprint' version of the P-47D. This was the P-47M that was in effect the production version of the XP-47J with the R-2800-57(C) radial engine and CH-5 turbocharger with a normal rating of 2,100hp (1,566kW) for take-off and at 38,750ft (11,810m) but a combat emergency rating of 2,800hp (2,088kW) at 32,500ft (9,905m). The new type was designed to cruise at medium altitude and, after acquiring its target, accelerate in a dive until it was close to the flying bomb, whereupon it would decelerate with the aid of air brakes, and open fire with its devastating fixed forward-firing battery of six or eight 0.5in (12.7mm) Browning machine-guns.

The type was pioneered by three YP-47M prototype

conversions from P-47D standard, and production totalled 130 aircraft that were dimensionally identical to the P-47D but otherwise differed in details such as empty weight of 10,423lb (4,728kg); normal take-off weight of 13,275lb (6,022kg); maximum take-off weight of 15,500lb (7,031kg); maximum level speed of 408kt (470mph; 756km/h) at 30,000ft (9,145m) declining to 347kt (400mph; 644km/h) at 10,000ft (3,048m); typical range of 486nm (560 miles; 901km) with internal fuel, and maximum climb rate at 5,000ft (1,524m) of 3,500ft (1,067m) per minute.

P-47N Thunderbolt: The last version of the Thunderbolt to be built, and a near contemporary of the P-47M, the P-47N was the largest and heaviest of all Thunderbolt variants. The type was designed for operations in the Pacific theatre with particular emphasis on the maximum possible range. Prefaced by a single XP-47N prototype conversion from P-47D standard, the P-47N was basically the P-47M with strengthened main landing gear units and wings of greater span and area. These wings also contained two fuel tanks to create a maximum internal capacity of 463 Imp gal (2,104.7 litres) that could be supplemented by one 91.6 Imp gal (416.4 litre) underfuselage tank and two 249.8 Imp gal (1,135.6 litre) underwing drop tanks. Even without the centreline tank, this gave the P-47N a range of 2,941nm (2,350 miles; 3,781km) and an endurance of 9 hours 36 minutes.

Production of the P-47N totalled 1,816 aircraft (1,667 of them from Farmingdale and 149 from Evansville), and all but the first 500 of these fighters had provision under their outer wing panels for up to ten zero-length launchers for 5in (127mm) rockets. The primary data for the P-47N included a fixed forward-firing armament of eight 0.5in (12.7mm) Browning machine-guns with 500 rounds per gun; disposable armament of two 1,000lb (454kg) bombs, or three 500lb (227kg) bombs, or ten 5in (127mm) HVAR rockets; span of 42ft 7in (12.98m) with an aspect ratio of 5.63 and an area of 322.00sq ft (29.91sq m); length of 36ft 4in (11.07m); height of 14ft 7in (4.445m); empty weight of 11,000lb (4,990kg); normal take-off weight of 16,300lb (7,394kg); maximum take-off weight of 20,700lb (9,390kg); maximum level speed of 399kt (460mph; 740km/h) at 27,000ft (8,230m) declining to 345kt (397mph; 639km/h) at 10,000ft (3,048m); typical range of 695nm (800 miles; 1,287km) with internal fuel, and maximum climb rate at 5,000ft (1,524m) of 2,770ft (844m) per minute.

Yakovlev Yak-9

Manufacturer: Yakovlev Design Bureau

Country of origin: USSR

Specification: Yak-9D

Type: Long-range fighter and fighter-bomber

Accommodation: Pilot in an enclosed cockpit

Entered service: November 1942

Left service: Mid-1950s

Operational equipment: standard communication and navigation equipment, plus a reflector gun sight

Armament: One 37mm 11P-37 fixed forward-firing cannon with 30 rounds in a moteur-canon installation and two 0.5in (12.7mm) Beresin UBS fixed forward-firing machine-guns with 110 rounds per gun in the upper part of the forward fuselage with synchronisation equipment to fire through the propeller disc, and up to 441lb (200kg) of disposable stores carried on two hardpoints (both under the wing with each unit rated at 220lb/100kg), and generally comprising two 220lb (100kg) FAB-100 bombs, or boxes of 5.5lb (2.5kg) PTAB-2.5 hollow-charge anti-tank bomblets, or six 3.2in (82mm) RS-82 air-to-surface rockets

Powerplant: One Klimov VK-105PF-3 Vee piston engine rated at 1240hp (924.5kW) for take-off

Fuel capacity: Internal fuel 147.4 Imp gal (670 litres) plus provision for 46.2 Imp gal (210 litres) of auxiliary fuel; external fuel none

Dimensions: Span 32ft 11.5in (9.74m); aspect ratio 5.53; area 184.61sq ft (17.15m²); length 27ft 10.67in (8.50m); height 9ft 10in (3.00m)

Weights: Empty 6107lb (2770kg) equipped; maximum take-off 6867lb (3115kg)

Seen over the Crimea in 1944, these are Yakovlev Yak-9D long-range fighters of a Guards fighter regiment. Nearest the camera is the aeroplane of Colonel Avdyeyev, a 15-victory ace.

Performance: Maximum level speed 'clean' 323kt (373mph; 600km/h) at 9845ft (3000m); maximum range 717nm (826 miles; 1330km); climb to 16,405ft (5000m) in 6 minutes 6 seconds; service ceiling 32,810ft (10,000m)

Variants
Yak-9: In the early part of its history, during 1940-41, the Yakovlev low-wing fighter series divided into two main development streams. One stream produced light fighters optimised for the battlefield air combat role, and its two most illustrious members were the Yak-1M and Yak-3; the other stream was based on the Yak-7DI with a measure of metal in its wing structure in a move that allowed an increase in internal fuel capacity and thus an optimisation for the longer-range role as exploited most successfully in the Yak-9. This had only relatively light firepower but was so successful that by 1944 it outnumbered all other Soviet fighters combined and then remained in production after the end of World War II (1939-45). The Yak-9 series was thus the most important and prolific of the derivatives stemming from the original Yak-1 fighter, and proved an exceptional type that was adapted for a number of roles.

As noted above, the type's immediate ancestor was the Yak-7, or rather its experimental Yak-7DI long-range fighter development, and from this the bureau evolved the Yak-9 a the production model with a wing capable of carrying a larger internal fuel load as a result of the replacement of the original type of wooden internal structure by a combination of steel and light alloy spars with light alloy and plywood ribs. Other changes introduced in the Yak-9 were a slightly larger rudder with a hinge line that was marginally less forward-swept, improved shaping of the engine coolant radiator and oil radiator ducts under the central fuselage and nose respectively, simpler trim tabs, balanced ailerons, the cockpit moved slightly farther to the rear, and a revised structure making greater use of light alloy.

Thus the oval-section fuselage was based on a primary structure of welded steel with a light alloy secondary structure for its forward and central sections, which were covered with light alloy panels and plywood respectively, while the rear fuselage was a semi-monocoque wood and plywood structure with a covering of plywood and fabric. The cantilever tail unit had plywood-covered wooden fixed surfaces and fabric-covered light alloy moving surfaces, and the wing was of mixed construction as detailed above. The wing was dihedraled, tapered in thickness and chord, and carried on its trailing edges the standard combination of outboard ailerons, which were of light alloy construction covered with fabric except on their light alloy leading edges, and inboard Shrenk-type split aps of light alloy construction. The airframe was completed by the cockpit, which was covered by a clear-view canopy with a rearward-sliding section for access and egress, and the fully retractable tailwheel landing gear, which included wide track main units that retracted inward under the power of a pneumatic system that was also used to operate the aps.

The type entered production in 1942 and was built in a number of important forms. The rst aircraft were delivered in October 1942 to a baseline standard that included a powerplant of one VK-105PF or VK-105PF-1 rated at 1180hp (880kW), tted with ejector exhaust stubs in a 1-2-2-1 arrangement on each side, and driving a three-blade VISh-61P propeller of the constant-speed type. The xed forward- ring armament comprised one 20mm ShVAK or MP-20 cannon with 120 rounds in a moteur-canon installation and either one 0.5in (12.7mm) Beresin UBS machine-gun with 200 rounds in the port side of the upper part of the forward fuselage with synchronisation equipment to re through the propeller disc, and there was also provision under the wings for two bombs or six rockets that were seldom carried as the Yak-9 was generally used in the pure ghter role.

The Yak-9 entered service in time for the strategically decisive Battle of Stalingrad that started in November 1942, and was in full service along the Eastern Front by February 1943, the month in which the ghting for Stalingrad ended with the destruction and/or capture of the German 6th Army. The other details of the Yak-9 in its basic form included an internal fuel capacity of 105.6 Imp gal (480 litres), span of 32ft 9.75in (10.00m) with an aspect ratio of 5.83 and an area of 184.61sq ft (17.15m†), length of 27ft 10.67in (8.50m), height of 8ft 0in (2.44m), empty weight of 4840lb (2200kg), maximum take-off weight of 6338lb (2875kg), maximum level speed of 322kt (371mph; 597km/h) at 13,125ft (4000m) declining to 287.5kt (331mph; 533km/h) at sea level, range of 432nm (497 miles; 800km), climb to 16,405ft (5000m) in 5 minutes 30 seconds, and service ceiling of 32,810ft (10,000m).

The Yak-9 was built in three factories, and by February 1943 all three had switched to an improved version of the baseline ghter with a revised wing. The original wing had been typi ed by its span of 32ft 9.75in (10.00m) with an aspect ratio of 5.83 and an area of 184.61sq ft (17.15m†), but the new wing spanned 32ft 11.5in (9.74m) with an aspect ratio 5.53 and an area of 184.61sq ft (17.15m†). The new wing introduced light alloy ribs and had blunter tips, although the area remained unaltered from that of the original type of wing. Further changes included a switch by April 1943 to the VK-105PF-2 or, more often, the VK-105PF-3 Vee engine rated at 1240hp (924.5kW) and driving a three-blade VISh-105S or VISh-105SV propeller of the constant-speed type. There were also some 15 different variations in armament introduced by the design bureau or as field modifications, and these included three 20mm ShVAK or MP-20 cannon including two in the wing leading edges, and schemes that included virtually every type of cannon in the Soviet inventory including the 23mm VYa and MP-23, the 37mm NS-37, OKB-16-37 and 11P-37, and the 45mm NS-45 weapons. It seems that none of these changes was signalled by a official modification of the basic designation with the possible exception of Yak-9M (Modifikatsirovannyi, or modified), a designation which was certainly applied in the field to fighters with a fixed forward-firing armament of one 20mm ShVAK cannon with 120 rounds and two 0.5in (12.7mm) UBS machine-guns with 150 rounds per gun.

Seen in mint condition after emerging from the production line at Kamensk-Uralsk during the late summer of 1942, this is a Yakovlev Yak-7A, a variant of the series that later introduced metal wing spars in an airframe based on that of the all-wood Yak-1, and thereby paved the way for the Yak-9 that was one of the USSR's finest fighters of World War II.

Yak-9D: This was the designation of the Dalnostnyi (long-range) escort fighter model introduced in the summer of 1943 with two additional but unprotected tanks in the wings to raise the overall capacity to 147.4 Imp gal (670 litres) or 193.6 Imp gal (880 litres) with the optional auxiliary tank under the cockpit.

Yak-9T: This Tankovyi (tank) designation was applied to the specialised anti-tank model that entered service early in 1943 with the cockpit moved back some 1ft 3.75in (0.40m) to preserve the centre of gravity in the right position despite the introduction of the heavy anti-tank cannon, the fuel capacity reduced to 79.2 Imp gal (360 litres), a moteur-canon installation of one 20, 23 or 37mm cannon firing armour-piercing projectiles, and provision for underwing containers of 5.5lb (2.5kg) PTAB hollow-charge anti-tank bomblets. The first Yak-9T flew in December 1942 with an armament of one 37mm 11P-37 cannon with 30 rounds and two 0.5in (12.7mm) UBS machine-guns with 100 rounds per gun, and the other production versions had one 20mm MP-20 cannon and two 0.5in (12.7mm) UBS machine-guns, or one 23mm VYa-23 cannon and one 0.5in (12.7mm) UBS machine-gun, or one 23mm MP-23-VV cannon and one 0.5in (12.7mm) UBS machine-gun.

The Yak-9T was built only in modest numbers, and its

details where different from those of the Yak-9D included a length of 27ft 11.5in (8.52m) increasing to 28ft 4.5in (8.65m) with the 37mm cannon, empty weight of 6063lb (2750kg), maximum take-off weight of 6746lb (3060kg), maximum level speed of 320kt (368.5mph; 593km/h) at 9845ft (3000m) declining to 287kt (330.5mph; 532km/h) at sea level, and range of 421nm (485 miles; 780km).

Yak-9K: This Krupnokalibernyi (heavy calibre) designation was applied to a specialised heavyweight anti-tank model, also known as the Yak-9-45, that was produced in small numbers during 1943 with a primary armament of one 45mm OKB-16-45 cannon with 15 rounds. The Yak-9K's details, where different from those of the Yak-9D, included a length of 29ft 1.25in (8.87m), empty weight of 6063lb (2750kg), maximum level speed of 309kt (356mph; 573km/h) at 9845ft (3000m) declining to 278.5kt (320.5mph; 516km/h) at sea level, range of 321nm (370 miles; 595km), climb to 16,405ft (5000m) in 5 minutes 42 seconds, and service ceiling of 29,530ft (9000m).

Yak-9B: This Bombardirovshchik (bomber) designation was applied to a special light bomber (really fighter-bomber) model produced in small numbers with a bay behind the cockpit for four 220lb (100kg) bombs or containers carrying 128 5.5lb (2.5kg) PTAB hollow-charge anti-tank bomblets. The reason for the development of a fighter-bomber version with internal bomb carriage was the result of the Yak-9 series' aversion to external loads, which made handling difficult, and the availability behind the pilot of an empty volume that was otherwise used for an instructor, passenger or freight in the Yak-7V model based on the same core fuselage structure. The first Yak-9B flew in December 1943, and the type entered limited service early in 1944 with a fixed forward-firing armament of one 20mm ShVAK cannon and one 0.5in (12.7mm) UBS machine-gun, or alternatively just the 0.5in (12.7mm) UBS machine-gun in the moteur-canon installation in place of the ShVAK.

Yak-9MPVO: This was the designation of a night-fighter model, also known as the Yak-9PVO (Protivo-Vozhduzhnoi Oborony, or air defence), produced in small numbers with a small searchlight in the leading edge of the port wing, and a radio compass in the rear fuselage, often under a transparent dorsal hatch.

Yak-9DD: This Dalnyi Deistviya (ultra long range) designation was given to a Yak-9D development for the very-range escort fighter role with increased fuel capacity and provision for a drop tank resulting in a range of 1187nm (1367 miles; 2200km). The type entered service in 1944, and was used for the escort of US Army Air Forces' Boeing B-17 flying Fortress and Consolidated B-24 Liberator heavy bombers operating against the Romanian oilfields at Ploiesti during 'shuttle' missions between Bari in southern Italy and Poltava in the Ukraine. The Yak-9DD's details, where different from those of the Yak-9D, included an empty weight of 6175lb (2801kg) and maximum take-off weight of 7275lb (3300kg).

Yak-9U: This Uluchshyennyi (improved) designation was applied to the second-generation fighter model of the Yak-9 series that entered service in June 1944 with an airframe thoroughly revised for reduced drag, a wing revised with a larger proportion of metal in its structure, and a powerplant of one VK-105PF-3 engine replaced from August 1944 by the Klimov VK-107A Vee piston engine rated at 1650hp (1230kW), fitted with individual ejector exhausts for a measure of thrust augmentation, and driving a three-blade VISh-107LO propeller of the constant-speed type; the version with the VK-107A engine had its wing moved 3.94in (0.10m) farther forward to keep the centre of gravity in the right position despite the adoption of the heavier engine.

As first flown in December 1943, the Yak-9U had a number of aerodynamic improvement to the cockpit canopy, rear fairing and rear fuselage to reduce drag, thicker plywood skinning on the rear fuselage for improved strength, a modified wing with rounded tips for greater span and area, the internal fuel capacity increased from 701 to 783lb (318 to 355kg), and completely redesigned cooling systems. These last now comprised an engine coolant radiator in a duct of larger cross section located farther back under the fuselage for centre of gravity and drag-reduction reasons, and a new oil cooler in the same position between the spars in the centre section but drawing its cooling air via an enlarged port wing-root inlet (that on the starboard side serving the supercharger) and exhausting the air via a flat and thrust-producing nozzle under the port wing root.

These changes provided a welcome increment in performance even with the original engine, and the Yak-9U entered production with a fixed forward-firing armament of one 20mm MP-20 cannon with 120 rounds and two 0.5in (12.7mm) UBS machine-guns with 170 rounds per gun. Other than those mentioned above, the features differentiating the Yak-9U from the Yak-9D were a span of 32ft 0.67in (9.77m) with an aspect ratio of 5.53 and an area of 185.68sq ft (17.25m≤), length of 28ft 0.67in (8.55m), height of 9ft 8.5in (2.96m) with the tail up, empty weight of 5677lb (2575kg), maximum take-off weight of 6393lb (2900kg), maximum level speed of 334.5kt (385mph; 620km/h) at 13,125ft (4000m) declining to 301kt (347mph; 558km/h) at sea level, range of 469.5nm (541 miles; 870km), climb to 16,405ft (5000m) in 4 minutes 48 seconds, and service ceiling of 34,120ft (10,400m).

In its improved form with the VK-107A engine, the Yak-9U was dimensionally identical to the Yak-9 with the VK-105PF-3 engine but differed in details such as its maximum take-off weight of 6830lb (3098kg), maximum level speed of 377kt (434mph; 698km/h) at 16,405ft (5000m) declining to 329kt (379mph; 610km/h) at sea level, climb to 16,405ft (5000m) in 3 minutes 48 seconds, and service ceiling of 39,040ft (11,900m).

Yak-9P: This Pushyechnyi (cannon) designation was accorded to a development of the Yak-9U with its fixed forward-firing armament increased to one 20mm MP-20 cannon in the moteur-canon installation and one or two 20mm ShVAK or MP-20 cannon in the upper part of the forward fuselage with synchronisation equipment to fire through the propeller disc. Powered by the VK-107A engine, the Yak-9P differed from the Yak-9U in details such as its span its 33ft 11.5in (10.35m) with an aspect ratio of 6.19 and an area of 186.22sq ft (17.30m≤), length of 28ft 6.9in (8.71m), empty weight of 5026lb (2280kg), maximum take-off weight of 6989lb (3170kg), maximum level speed of 360.5kt (415mph; 668km/h) at 16,405ft (5000m), climb to 16,405ft (5000m) in 3 minutes 6 seconds, and service ceiling of 40,025ft (12,200m).

Production of the Yak-9 series ended in August 1945 after the completion of the 16,769 aircraft including more than 3900 of the Yak-9U conversion trainer and its relatives.